ROOF OVER BRITAIN

THE OFFICIAL STORY OF THE A.A DEFENCES, 1939–1942

A GAMES.

NINEPENCE NET

HOSTILE
AIRCRAFT

OBSERVER
POST

RADIO LOCATION

ANTI-AIRCRAFT
OPERATIONS
ROOM

BALLOON COMMAND

BALLOON SITES
OVER TARGET

FIGHTER
GROUP H.Q.

▲

ROOF

OVER BRITAIN

THE OFFICIAL STORY OF BRITAIN'S

ANTI-AIRCRAFT DEFENCES 1939-1942

Prepared for
THE WAR OFFICE
and
THE AIR MINISTRY
by
THE MINISTRY OF INFORMATION

1943

LONDON: HIS MAJESTY'S STATIONERY OFFICE

CONTENTS

PRICE 9D. NET

To be purchased from His Majesty's Stationery Office at : York House, Kings-
way, London, W.C.2 ; 120 George Street, Edinburgh, 2 ; 39–41 King Street,
Manchester, 2 ; 1 St. Andrew's Crescent, Cardiff ; 80 Chichester Street, Belfast ;
or through any bookseller.   Wt. 1943.   W.P.Ltd.   S.O. Code No. 70–418*.

ILLUSTRATIONS

There are many men and women in the Forces who would welcome a chance of reading this book. If you hand it in to the nearest Post Office, it will go to them.

Printed in Great Britain by The Whitefriars Press Ltd., London and Tonbridge.

Foreword

THIS BOOK supplements and continues the story of how the R.A.F. defeated the attack of the German Air Force during the autumn of 1940. Much of the air fighting has already been described in " The Battle of Britain." But the fighter squadrons never constituted the whole of our defensive system. It has therefore been thought worth-while to give some account of the other materials which went to the making of the " Roof over Britain " ; and the War Office and Air Ministry have combined to tell the story of the static defences—A.A. guns, searchlights, balloons and the Royal Observer Corps. Captain Anthony Cotterell was kindly lent by the Army Bureau of Current Affairs to write the Army part of the story and the Air Ministry compiled the story of the balloons.

At the beginning of the war the roof was only a fairly tough framework. With the exception of Germany, no nation in the world at that time had an even approximately complete system of anti-aircraft defences ; we were certainly, after—a long way after—Germany, the best prepared. Moreover, one of the most creditable parts of the story is the speed at which our defences were developed. The Prime Minister has well described the character of a munitions programme :—" The first year—nothing at all ; the second year—very little ; the third year—quite a lot ; the fourth year—all you want." If September 1938, with its rather humiliating improvisations, be taken as the starting date, it will be seen that the development of our anti-aircraft defences has been better than scheduled. So this story is worth telling as a story of efficiency.

It is worth telling for another reason. Though their story is not dull, the life and the work of the men and women of the static defences very often contains every element of exasperation. They have had to fight the canker of armies, monotony—often in isolated stations far from their own homes and from anybody's home. Their victory over monotony is described in these pages.

The reader will observe that there are holes in the story, though not in the roof. Just as the static defences were complementary by day to our fighter squadrons, so by night they are complementary to our night-fighters. Some stories of the exploits of night-fighters have been published in the Press, and have told the enemy only what they already know—namely, that our night-fighters are as skilled and courageous as other sections of the R.A.F. But exactly how night-fighters bring the enemy down would be most useful knowledge, and must be denied to him.

Again, since the book deals with the A.A. Defences of Great Britain, no mention has been made of the large numbers of trained A.A. regiments supplied by A.A. Command for service overseas. It is worth noting, however, that the roof over Britain was built simultaneously with roofs over many other places. Some of the strain has recently been taken by the Home Guard, whose progressively more valuable work must also be reserved for fuller and separate treatment.

Some readers may think there is another gap in the story, because it does not deal in any way with the Civil Defences. This gap has been deliberately left. The Civil Defences have their own story to tell, and a magnificent one it is—so magnificent that they have been left to tell it themselves.

1. "It isn't easy to shoot down a 'plane"

ON A NIGHT in March, 1941, the Battery Commander responsible for the A.A. defence of the Widnes area made out the following incident report :—

" **21.25 hours**—An aircraft blew up in the air, bearing 290.
" **21.30 hours**—An aircraft was seen surrounded by a shell burst and lit up with an orange glow.
" **21.35 hours**—An aircraft crashed in flames, bearing 240—distance about 3 miles."

The 'plane referred to in the last two extracts, a Heinkel III, pitched in a sports field on the town's outskirts. It burned luridly, consuming the pilot ; but three members of the crew who baled out were captured. The 'plane had first been hit by an anti-aircraft shell, causing loss of height and speed ; then a night-fighter had picked it up and fired from point-blank range ; and finally, when its fall had become a scream of punctured engines, the 'plane had struck a barrage balloon cable.

That is an example of the Air Defence of Great Britain—A.D.G.B. —in the full flower of co-operative function. Fighter Command is the main defence of Britain ; but Fighter Command could not survive without A.A. Command, and that is what we are concerned with here—the story of our anti-aircraft guns and searchlights.

It isn't easy to shoot down a 'plane with an anti-aircraft gun. With a field gun, sitting still, shooting at a fixed target, mathematically you only expect one hit in a hundred rounds. There are several reasons why this should be so ; for instance, atmospheric conditions, such as a belt of moisture, deflect the shell in its flight ; and with each shot the charge burns a little differently.

The anti-aircraft problem is more complicated. Instead of sitting still, the target is moving at anything up to 300 m.p.h. with the ability to alter course left or right, up or down. If the target is flying high it may take 20 or 30 seconds for the shell to reach it, and the gun must be laid a corresponding distance ahead. Moreover the range must be determined so that the fuse can be set, and above all, this must be done continuously so that the gun is always laid in the right direction. When you are ready to fire, the 'plane, though its engines sound immediately overhead, is actually two miles away. And to hit it with a shell at that great height the gunners may have to aim at a point two miles farther still. Then, if the raider does not alter course or height, as it naturally does when under fire, the climbing shell and the bomber will meet. In other words the raider, which is heard apparently overhead at the Crystal Palace, is in fact at that moment over Dulwich ; and the shell which is fired at the Crystal Palace must go to Parliament Square to hit it. It is like shooting a pheasant with a rifle in the dark. Perfect team work is necessary. Any single man, from the man who sees the 'plane and decides it is hostile (a testingly responsible decision), to the man who pulls the firing lever, can wreck the shoot.

So it is not bad going that three times our A.A. gunners have shot down more than 50 German 'planes over this country in a week, and that during one week they shot down 70. During their most successful 24 hours, August 15th, 1940, they destroyed 23 enemy 'planes, this bag being contributed to by gun batteries in seven towns from Dundee to Dover. Eleven were brought down at Dover, seven on Tyneside and Teeside, and the rest at Southampton, Harwich and Dundee.

A fortnight later, on August 31st, 21 were shot down, 16 of them in 90 minutes during the evening blitz. During the whole of 1940, A.A. batteries in the British Isles shot down $444\frac{1}{2}$ enemy aircraft. The odd half represents the A.A. gunners' share in an enemy bomber which was finished off by fighters after it had been winged by a near miss from a ground battery. These figures do not include the many probables which limp out over the coast and crash unwitnessed in the sea.

During the first two years of war just on 600 'planes were shot down by A.A. fire over this country, and during the same two years fighter 'planes destroyed 3,900. So, roughly speaking, the guns bring down one 'plane for every six shot down by fighters. The ratio varies. In March and April, 1941, it was one to the guns and two to the fighters. Every third aircraft shot down was shot down by the guns.

To disturb the aim and deter the faint-hearted

A more important criterion of efficiency is how our A.A. fire compares with the German A.A. fire. This is a difficult question to answer.

But certainly it is true that our bomber losses are lower than the enemy's *known* losses in proportion to the number of 'planes used. Let us take one example of our losses in man-power, for the loss of trained crews is in every way more serious than the loss of machines. In the big four-figure raid on Cologne, the target was attacked by about 6,000 men (slightly less than the bayonet strength of a Division of infantry). They suffered between 300 and 400 casualties only. This in spite of the fact that our bombers usually attack at lower heights than the enemy in order to ensure greater accuracy, and in consequence tend to provide better targets than the German bombers over here. In contrast, on the great day of September 15th, 1940, the Germans attacked with between 2,000 and 3,000 men, and lost between 600 and 700 of them.

German respect for our A.A. defences started low but has flourished and grown. The first-class enemy pilots keep on with their job, the others don't. If a man is wondering whether he has got to take avoiding action he is not going to concentrate on hitting Buckingham Palace or the War Office ; he is going to be jinking about, and his aim will be disturbed at a critical moment. That is one of the main functions of Anti-Aircraft Command—to disturb the aim and deter the faint-hearted. The number of planes shot down is by no means the only measure of anti-aircraft efficiency and value.

Life is easy when there are plenty of 'planes to shoot down ; it is not so obviously worth while to men who have had to wait months, perhaps years, for the opportunity to fire at an enemy 'plane at all. Months, or years, of the most demoralising dullness, during every hour of which it is necessary to behave as if the enemy were expected at any minute. And when, finally, the enemy 'plane does arrive, it may be only possible to fire at it for a few seconds ; or, perhaps, because our own 'planes are in the neighbourhood, they may not be allowed to fire at all.

Conditions of life in the A.A. Command are much more difficult than is generally imagined even by the rest of the Army. The men must be in constant and instant readiness, all through the day ;

some of them all through the day and night ; some of them all through the night with maintenance work during the day. They are in little pockets all over the country, many of them under junior N.C.Os. and miles from the nearest farmhouse. A few, even at this stage of the war, have not yet had the chance to fire their guns. It is therefore a dull life and must often seem a meaningless one, full of petty, and sometimes not so petty, hardships and discomforts. This book is an account of their work and the trials they have to face, and an appreciation of their achievement.

2. The Building of the Roof

THE TASK of developing A.A. defences is not new. It had to be done in the last war. But the job in 1914 was very different from the job in 1939. In 1914 there was no semblance of a black-out until October 1st, and on that day 12 A.A. guns and 12 searchlights were deployed in the London Area. These merely token defences were not so inadequate as they seemed, because air-power was in its infancy ; and the attack was unlikely to be more terrible than the defence. But the Germans were already thinking of terror raids.

In September, 1914, the Chief of the German Naval Staff wrote a minute saying, " I hold the view that we should leave no means untried to crush England, and that successful air raids on London, in view of the already existing nervousness of the people, would prove a valuable means to that end." On January 9th, 1915, the Kaiser gave his permission for attacks to start, these attacks to be " expressly restricted to military shipyards, arsenals, docks, and, in general, military establishments ; London itself was not to be bombed."

When the raids came they caused a great loss of working time and not a little upset. The first place to be bombed—King's Lynn on January 19th, 1915—was the subject of a report from the Zeppelin commander to the effect that he had been " heavily attacked by guns and engaged by searchlights." Such defences, however, did not exist, and his report gives some indication of his diffidence. Nevertheless, these comparatively feeble raids had a considerable effect, not only in slowing up munition production but in keeping back from France sorely needed fighter aircraft and A.A. guns. Gradually the defences got the upper hand ; the beginning of the end of the Zeppelins came when Leefe Robinson earned his V.C. by shooting down the SL.11 near Cuffley. Soon the Germans were routeing themselves clear of the London defences.

By 1918 these consisted of 284 guns, 377 searchlights, and 11 fighter squadrons. But in 1919 A.D.G.B. was disbanded, and until 1922 there was no A.A. protection in this country except for one very small regular brigade and searchlight battalion—2/3,000 men in all. In 1922, four heavy Anti-Aircraft Regiments (then called brigades) and two searchlight battalions were formed, all in and around London. Most of their recruits came from the Banks, the Insurance Companies, Lloyd's, and one or two large concerns like Vickers and the Wandsworth Gas Company. They were very much under strength and recruiting was a problem they could not solve. At the first post-war camps in 1923 there were about 30 men to represent batteries which should have had 150 men. Certainly there was little enough inducement to join except for the incorrigibly military or determinedly sociable. They had to spend a great deal of their first camp period in humping ammunition over two and a half miles of sand dunes. They not only carried their own ammunition, but that of the regulars who followed them to camp, and they had next to no transport. Practice was thus negligible.

They went to camp again the following year, much increased in strength, but still saddled with so many fatigues that they had little time for shooting. Equipment was meagre in the extreme, money was always tight, and it was not unusual for units to spend considerable sums of money in buying their own equipment.

By 1925 the political situation started to look less favourable, and very slowly a start was made to rebuild the air defences. There were now two regular anti-aircraft brigades—about 5,000 men—who spent half their year running camps for territorials. The regulars were not designed for the defence of this country but to go abroad with an expeditionary force. Things gradually began to build up ; by 1936 there was one A.A. Division, and a second Division was formed. By 1938 there were five, and they were brought together under one A.A. Corps. In 1939 there were seven Divisions and the Corps became a Command.

This seems a lot compared with 1914 ; but no comparison is valid. Only eight months later the German Air Force killed 30,000 people in Rotterdam in half an hour. In September 1939, an air attack on any one of the countless targets crowded into this island was not only possible but considered highly probable. The 1939 establishment was therefore by no means excessive. Moreover, the greater part of the men were recent recruits, and the later flood of new or renovated guns was still only a trickle. This makes it the more remarkable that a year later a formidable artillery served by fully skilled gun-crews was ready to meet the assault of the *Luftwaffe*.

Credit for this jump from infancy to maturity must be shared among many people, from the men and women who made the guns and shells to the General who controlled the destinies of A.A. Command. General Sir Frederic Pile, who took over this job a few weeks before the outbreak of war, has made the family created by his predecessor grow with an efficiency and energy for which both his command and the public have good cause to be grateful. The modern commander has an administrative job which would tax the talents of a captain of industry, on top of a military job which is always presenting new possibilities and problems. He has to consider everything from the finding of labour to build huts for the A.T.S. to the fragmentation of metals under certain conditions. To revive an echo of a conundrum of 1914-18 vintage, though bread is the staff of life, the life of the staff is no longer a long loaf.

Part of the success of A.A. Command is due to the fact that General Pile has known how to get the best out of his staff and that he has been to scientists the kind of patron they dream about. All their ideas have been tried at least once, and tried quickly. That is why in so short a time the basis of our A.A. defences has been changed from a bluff to a buckler.

Studying the enemy's methods

As part of the process of trying to keep one jump ahead of the enemy, officers from A.A. Command have often flown with our bomber crews. These officers are not in any sense passengers ; they are trained as air gunners, but their main job is to observe and report on the enemy's ground defences and how they can be best avoided, and to see what lessons can be learned from the enemy.

The officers originally chosen were sent on a short course at a Searchlight Wing, where their knowledge of searchlight methods was brought up-to-date and amplified.

But the main emphasis of the course was on cultivating their powers of observation. For instance, they were set down on a hillside, each with binoculars, and told to observe and comment on events in a small barbed-wire encampment some distance away. A man came out of the camp and sat down reading a newspaper which reflected brightly and would give away the position from the air. An A.T.S. girl came up to the camp, spoke to the sentry and was admitted. Rifle fire broke out in some woods near by and the camp was captured.

The class had to write a reconstruction of these and the other events ; and they had to draw a panorama of the scene showing how they would have attacked the camp, and why. All this, of course, was designed to build up the spirit of restless inquisitiveness which is the body and soul of reconnaissance. They were taken out at night and shown what all kinds of searchlights looked like, and then they were sent on a three-day course in which guns were fired at a point near them to train them to distinguish the different kinds of fire. They were then posted to R.A.F. operational training units for a further course in air gunnery. Here they learned to operate aircraft guns and turrets. They learned to cure gun stoppages and write reports sitting in the dark in a confined space. They had to practise in a turret in a dark room until they passed the tests. It was a condensed air gunner's course, without radio, but thorough enough to entitle them to wear the air gunner's single wing badge.

Immediately afterwards they were posted to different Bomber stations and joined their crews. The air observer sits in the front gunner's turret. To get into it he clambers over the bomb-aimer's panel, opens the bulkhead door and the two turret doors and swings himself in by a bar in the roof of the turret. There is not much room to move about. The seat is just large enough and placed between two ammunition tanks on which he can rest his elbows during the flight. There are little holes in the top of the tank through which you can see the ammunition being fed into the guns.

The guns are at eye level with a ring sight in between them. To rotate the turret and fire the guns the observer has two handles worked on rather the same principle as the handle-bars of a motor-cycle. When you twist the handles the turret swings round, and to fire the guns there is a trigger appendage to the grips.

The air observers are not usually instructed to look for anything in particular, but to make a general and detailed report of everything they see. On a clear night they may be able to study the enemy's fire control methods and searchlight deployment for more than half an hour while approaching the target, and they achieve impressively detailed results when they are under fire. On the first few trips their impressions tend to be sketchy, but with each flight they become more valuable. Time is the important thing ; if they know exactly what time a thing happened they can check with the navigator afterwards exactly where it was on the ground. They jot their notes by a dim orange lamp which shines over their shoulder.

Here are typical extracts from reports made by one officer who is forty years old ; before the war he was an electrical engineer. These extracts are, of course, necessarily jumbled.

" The gun flashes on the ground were of two distinct and definite colours, *i.e.*, yellow and deep orange. As far as we could see, the latter were from the very heavy guns."

" As far as we could see the guns were not being directed but were firing a barrage at all heights from 12,000-18,000 feet."

" Very small number of guns, probably not more than 10 of, say, 88-mm. calibre. There was no obvious form of fire control being used. The shells were bursting in all parts of the sky above the target, and at all heights between 14,000-16,000 feet, but none near enough to cause us any anxiety."

Some hundreds of scientists

What are these reports used for ? They go to Bomber Command and are sometimes used in briefing crews who make subsequent raids on the same area. They go to the military intelligence directorate to confirm or amplify their other sources of information about the same areas. They go to the men who plan our own A.A. defences ; and—perhaps most interesting of all—they go to the scientists, to the A.A. Command's Operations Research Group.

A.A. Command has two main research stations devoted entirely to its problems and employing some hundreds of scientists. The Operations Research Group consists of about 70 scientists and statisticians who work in a three-storied suburban vicarage and overflow into two small army huts.

The air observers' reports are dealt with mainly by the statisticians. If the observer reports 14 illuminations over Brest and gives an estimate of the number of searchlights visible over a certain area, the statisticians may then be able to work out the density and extent of the searchlight belt. The scientists have more than one observer's report to go on, of course. There were eight on the first Paris raid as well as all the R.A.F. reports. But naturally the A.A. officers, with their gunnery experience, can usually provide a better picture of ground defences than the airmen. Suppose the observers' reports suggest that the enemy are using some new kind of equipment ; this intelligence might be the basis of a raid on the enemy coasts.

Perhaps an observer may report the use of red and blue searchlights. Under certain weather conditions this may be an illusion produced by ordinary white lights. But, if the same lights are reported in the same places on different nights in different weather, it is worth investigating.

Perhaps we have rather exaggerated the impact of the observers' reports on the scientists' work, the value and extent of which it is difficult to over-estimate. The scientists also do their own field work. They have recording units which go and stay with the guns. The units consist of five men and a recording van. They test their theories and designs as translated into action.

Since the war started the progress in research and its results have been great. The guns themselves are much the same, but the methods of fire control have advanced as far as the Rolls-Royce from the hansom cab.

3. The Men who Also Serve

A N Y   A C C O U N T   of how A.A. defences developed must include the story of the Royal Observer Corps. This is how its members live and work.

Two men stand in a sand-bagged emplacement built high on a hill to give an unbroken view. The evening is completely quiet, but they are listening hard. The wild fowl on the marsh below have been agitating, and that is often the first hint of a Heinkel.

One man wears head-phones, with a mouthpiece strapped over his chest. The other is working a plotting instrument, which stands on a tripod in the centre of the post. It consists of a round dial, marked with numbers and squares. On top of this is a height finder.

Their observations are reported into the telephone rather as follows : '' Seen. 5678. South-east. Eight. At 10,000.'' This means that they have seen 'planes approaching over the square denoted by 5678 on their charts, that they are headed south-east, that they are eight in number and flying at 10,000 feet. They also report the type of 'plane. More often than not the 'plane is friendly, but reports are made just the same. The observers can recognise almost any 'plane without thinking twice, and their accuracy at estimating heights is uncannily good.

There are 1,400 of these posts manned by men and women, mostly part-time workers, who give what time they can spare from their normal work. It is not always pleasant, for they cannot take shelter however bad the weather is, nor can they have a fire because it would be seen from the air.

Plenty of mistakes can be made. A certain kind of railway-carriage dynamo sounds like a distant air-raid siren, and the hum of a factory or a motor-boat engine can be extraordinarily like the intermittent drone of a 'plane.

The telephone which one of the observers wears connects the post to a centre. Here a crew of men and women sit round a table on which is a large-scale map of the area, broken up into squares and sub-divided into the smaller, numbered squares as at the posts. Each member wears head-phones with a mouth-piece strapped over his chest and is in direct contact with three of the posts.

When a post reports the presence of an aircraft, a coloured counter is put into the appropriate square. As the aircraft is reported to have moved, so the counter follows it.

Above the table, on a platform, are the tellers. Watching the table, they report the movements on the chart to fighter groups, airfields and other defence centres responsible for the reception of the enemy. Friendly and enemy 'planes have different designations, and from a glance at the chart you can see their relative positions. As the raiders move out of the area the neighbouring centres are warned of their approach. Whether you are friend or enemy they are tracking you all the time. The Royal Observer Corps have been on watch night and day without a break since August 24th, 1939.

Tying the system together

Another girder of the " roof over Britain " is the work of the Royal Corps of Signals. The whole system of defence is based on first-class communications—on telling the gunners what is happening so that they can make arrangements for what is likely to happen somewhere else. The whole A.A. Command is a network of communication. Each gun and searchlight site is connected with its gun-operations room and its neighbours. Gun and Light sites, observer posts, operations rooms, fighter sectors and airfields are all inter-connected in a maze of telephone cables, supplemented by despatch riders and radio. The Post Office telephone and telegraph system has been used as a basis. To its thousands of miles of wire, stretching to every corner of the country, have been added hundreds of miles of field lines and new circuits. For each circuit there are alternatives planned in case of emergency. Even the location of private phones is noted, so that, if need be, they can be taken over and used.

When the raids come, the cables are liable to get broken. Then the line parties of the Royal Corps of Signals have to get to work, often in extremely difficult conditions, tracing and repairing the breakdowns. Here is the story of one of these excursions, which happened during the attacks on London.   It concerns a certain gun site on the Isle of Dogs.

The line party, consisting of a subaltern, and two trucks each carrying about ten men and loaded with the usual signals paraphernalia—cables, poles, ladders, lengths of spun yarn, climbing irons and cable barrows for paying out cable, got their orders at 9.30 a.m.

It took quite a time to drive down to the Isle of Dogs through all the deviations caused by bombs which had exploded, or were expected to explode.

The Isle of Dogs is not a natural island, but a tongue of land moulded by a U-bend in the Thames and isolated by ramifications of docks.   Silhouetted by the river, it was a natural target, and the warehouses and working-class housing which crowded it had taken a terrible battering.   The fires were still burning, and across the river the Surrey Docks were burning too.

There was one approach left open by which the signals lorries could approach the gun site, and this was stopped a hundred yards before the site by a large bomb crater.   The site was ringed with craters, so it was impossible to get a lorry on to it.

In the ordinary way a line party works its way along the cables, repairing them where they are broken.   But the cables to this gun site had been laid mostly underground and partly under water. They had been laid by the G.P.O., who in the ordinary way would be responsible for their maintenance ; but, as may be imagined, the G.P.O. were not entirely disengaged that morning.   There was no possibility of getting such a complicated job done, and it was urgently necessary to restore communications by nightfall.   The only way was to lay an entirely new cable to the nearest telephone exchange, which was two miles away by direct route, and, allowing for diversions, likely to be nearly twice as far.

There was no time to carry the cable properly on poles ; they had to lay it along the gutter, leaving signalmen at intervals to guard it. It was a hot day, and though the fires were still burning, it was strangely quiet.   The streets were deserted, like those of a wild-west ghost town.   The little shops were there, with goods in the window but no one in the back room waiting to sell them.   Every so often they came to a warehouse on fire and they had to estimate how far to allow for the fire to spread before laying the cable.   Mostly they laid it along the gutter, but sometimes over the ruins of a building, and once over the swing bridge of a dock.   The sirens went several times, but nothing serious developed.   They plodded on, round warehouses, under cranes, across scrap-iron yards, scrub-land, dock-railway lines, under fences, over bridges. The air was laden with smoke, dust and filth. The men were filthy and sweating with the heat and annoyance of having to make constant diversions to avoid delayed-action bombs, which in those days were much more incalculable dangers than they are now.

Working at great pressure the men finally got the line through at 4 p.m. When it came to testing it, they weren't at all sure that it would work. But it did, and just as the voice came through, the sirens announced the first of the night's attacks.

Being a despatch rider isn't much fun during a heavy raid. With the breaking down of communications, despatch riders are over-worked taking messages to sites. All the troubles of driving a car through the rubble, clay and water of a bombed area are multiplied many times on a motor bike. You have greater mobility, but much greater discomforts. The compensating factor is that, owing to the acuteness of these discomforts, you quickly lose most of your capacity for apprehension, and develop a certain bitter relish for setbacks.

During the Coventry attacks one D.R., L-Cpl. Sidney Slight, was visiting an ammunition dump when a bomb landed near by and blew him a dozen yards. He recovered his bike and a few minutes later his tyre was burst open by splinters. He exchanged his wheel for one taken from another bike, and musing on what the owner would say when he came to use his bike, he set off again. He drove up one road, and five minutes later made the return journey. An army truck saved him from a nasty spill, for seeing its shape in the darkness he pulled up to avoid it, and found it was wedged in a bomb crater which hadn't been there five minutes before and into which he would have pitched.

A London D.R., Signalman Hoy, was less lucky. He drove into a bomb crater and found himself practically buried in wet slimy clay. A policeman came to help him out and fell in himself, wearing a brand new uniform. Another D.R. fell off his bike 18 times in 40 minutes, and when he arrived, found he was due to go on guard in 35 minutes' time.

The Ordnance men must work

The other great supporting arm of A.A. Command is the Royal Army Ordnance Corps, which supplies and maintains all the guns and instruments, all the lights and all the generating sets.

This has been built up from as near nothing as made little differ-ence. When the war started there were only a few sets of hand tools to maintain the A.A. defences of London. But the R.A.O.C. men not only did their own work, but often other people's as well. For instance, there was a great shortage of striker pins, which strike the cartridge and detonate the charge. As mass raids were expected to start any time, it was essential that we should be able to fire what shells we had from any guns that had so far been delivered. But there was no way of getting striker pins except for the R.A.O.C. to make them. They did this by rescuing an ancient hand-driven lathe which had been condemned as useless, and working it night and day.

Individual initiative has been the keynote all along. Some R.A.O.C. men were fixing fire-control instruments, which involved taking a cable along a pipe leading through a concrete emplacement. But there was a kink in the pipe too steep to thread the cable through. They solved this problem by borrowing a local ferret and sending it through the pipe with a piece of string tied to one leg and then pulling the cable through at the end of the string.

When the raids started the work of maintenance became urgent and arduous in the extreme. After every substantial engagement the guns and instruments must be examined and checked. This is highly technical work and it means a tremendous amount of work for the limited numbers of R.A.O.C. men.

4. The First Winter

A T 9.20 in the morning of October 16th, 1939, the Gun Operations Room in the Forth Area started to record the approach of enemy aircraft. All the morning these plots continued, the aircraft flying very high and obviously out on reconnaissance. When they were seen by gun crews, which was rarely, they were too high to be positively identified, and as they were only isolated 'planes, no fire was opened. At twenty-seven minutes past two that afternoon, operators in the Forth Gun Operations Room were astonished to see a red light flash up, meaning " Guns in Action." No warning of any sort had been received, and no sirens had sounded. They immediately sent out the order " Action " to all sites, and almost at that moment enemy aircraft appeared over the Forth Bridge. No attempt was made to bomb the bridge itself ; the Germans were trying for two warships lying near it, and for another coming up the Forth.

A gun site south of the Forth was busily engaged in gun drill when suddenly the spotters saw what was unmistakably a German aircraft approaching the Forth Bridge.   Hurriedly the crew changed their dummy ammunition for live, while their instruments were laid on the 'planes.   Before they could open fire it had dived too low, but another had appeared from the clouds.   This time the gunners were more fortunate and shot a large portion of the Nazi's tail-plane down into the Firth of Forth.   This raider was finished off by a Spitfire, and crashed into the sea off Port Seton.   This Heavy A.A. Battery was the first Anti-Aircraft Battery to help in bringing down an enemy raider over this country.

Meanwhile, all neighbouring gun sites were hurriedly going into action.   The raiders, between six and nine in number, flew over from the coast well to the south of their target, at heights of 12,000-15,000 feet.   They then turned north, and making good use of cloud cover, descended to about 4,000 feet before diving on their target. All the attacks were made independently and from different directions.   After their dive attack they would fly off as low as 50 feet, making it impossible for the heavy gunners to continue firing.   In spite of this another plane was damaged by A.A. fire and our fighters accounted for two more.

Meanwhile a report had come in that a number of biplanes, said to be Henschel 123s, were off the coast near Dunbar ; probably a ruse to draw off our fighters.

For nearly two hours on and off the attack continued, until, soon after four o'clock the last of the raiders disappeared, pursued by our fighters.   No bombs fell on land or on the dockyard, but a few casualties and some slight damage were suffered by the ships.

Lessons were learned from this raid, which was the first chance of trying out the effect of anti-aircraft fire and fighters in action together.   The fighters reported that the bursts of anti-aircraft fire were of great assistance in locating the enemy.   Gunners found that the great superiority in speed of the Spitfire over a German bomber made it difficult to know when to stop firing at an enemy 'plane being pursued by a Spitfire.

So our Ack-Ack gun crews, not altogether displeased with their day's work, and well content with being the lucky ones to draw first blood, collected their empty shell cases and hoped the enemy would return.

A.A. Guns in the Shetlands

The Shetlands were the first part of the British Isles to be bombed and there was a song to celebrate the event.   The title of the song, `` Run, Rabbit, Run,'' referred to the only casualty sustained during the raid. It was clear that some A.A. defence was required—though not, of course, for the rabbits, which already had shelters.

The guns landed one mild day in January 1940. Battery head-quarters was established and the guns were sent immediately to their sites in a remote corner of the island some 30 miles away. The crews settled down in what accommodation they could find, and started to dig their gun positions by day and think of ways of keeping out the cold by night.

Before their arrival the Germans had come frequently, so they had high hopes of almost daily action. Nothing of the kind occurred. There was one raid soon after arrival, but no more for many weeks. This is recorded merely as a coincidence, but to the Shetlanders it was much more. The gunners' prestige soared.

Most of the gunners were Yorkshiremen, with a sprinkling of young Scots. They were short of men and there was no question of leave, not even a few hours in Lerwick.

The local people depended for their living on Shetland wool. The women walked along carrying great baskets of peat on their backs and knitting all the time. At night the gunners would go into the cottages and drink tea. The Northern Lights were magnificent ; the men could have read the newspapers at midnight if they had had any newspapers.

The social event of the week on each site was the visit of an E.N.S.A. Film Unit. It was a godsend to everybody. The apparatus was rigged up in a hut, and the shows were open to Shetlanders. They came from miles around, by every possible means of conveyance except Shetland ponies, of which there seemed to be very few. Many of the islanders had never seen a film before and never seen a train. Afterwards they would push back the benches, sprinkle French chalk on the floor, and dancè to music from the Film Unit's sound apparatus. Most of the Shetlanders only knew their own reels, but the gunners soon introduced them to the cultural advances of the mainland.

Probably the temperature in Shetland was no lower than on the mainland. It was the wind that made it so bitter. There were times when it was impossible to stand up.

Like all A.A. units, they had the problem of how to fill spare time in the evenings, when the work was finished, but they were tied down to the site. In some ways this is an easier matter in really lonely places than it is when the men are tantalisingly near the amenities of a big town but might as well be in the Shetlands for all the chance there is of getting to them. On really lonely sites the gunners know they must provide their own entertainment and so settle down to

doing it.   Some odd little institutions sprang up.   At one site a
club was formed which called itself the " Ding-Bats."   The
members made nonsensical remarks and generally behaved (off
parade) as if they were fey.   It was a sort of inoculation against
insanity.   There were also the usual spelling bees, language classes
and debates, and an occasional concert with the villagers as audience.
Add to this the most important of all occupations of service men in
lonely places—reading letters, writing letters, and looking forward
to receiving letters.

The Searchlights settle in

The Shetlanders were glad to welcome the gunners.   Not all
communities are so enthusiastic.   Take the case of a certain Searchlight Battery—neither typical nor extraordinary.   A searchlight site
was erected about half a mile from a village, and the inhabitants,
partly farmers, partly miners, were perturbed.   They had never been
bombed and they felt that with the arrival of the searchlights they
very well might be.   So they held an indignation meeting and sent
a letter of protest to the War Office.   To aggravate matters, the only
billet that could be found for the troops, until their huts were built,
was the village hall where all the social events were normally held.

But the men were determined, by their behaviour, to fight this
hostility and they did so to such purpose that, instead of pursuing
their protest to the War Office, the villagers gave them a twelve-
guinea wireless set.   In no time at all the troop clerk became
engaged to the daughter of the local policeman, and when the huts
were finished the villagers sent presents of furniture.

Shortly after, the expected bomb did fall.   It was not a big one,
and it did not land on the village : it landed about 100 yards from
the site, where it made quite a mess of the cookhouse.   Nobody was
hurt, but next morning the entire village turned out to see if any
help was needed.

Then the battery was moved a matter of 50 miles.   Another
protest meeting was held, another letter sent to the War Office, this
time protesting against the removal.   But it was as much in vain
as the first one.   However, the link was not broken.   The village
hired a coach, travelled the 50 miles, taking comforts, cigarettes,
etc., and a party was held at the new site.

One Searchlight Battery, made up largely of townsmen, found
their first war-station to be in one of the most isolated parts of
Britain, on the bleak, lonely Derbyshire peaks.   They arrived in
icy, snowy weather in a tiny village which consisted of one street,
about 90 inhabitants and a handful of houses.

The village was on top of a hill so steep that it took only 20 minutes to walk down it to the nearest real village, but 55 minutes of hard walking to get back. A five-mile route march, once a week, was necessary in order to have a bath.

The site which the troops had to build was four miles away from the village where the men were billeted. This necessitated a march every morning with picks, spades and wheel-barrow. Although the site was so high, no sign of human habitation could be seen except an occasional lonely farmhouse. The men were cheered up to discover that opposite their site was what seemed a flourishing farm. But from the start the farmer put up a " Not Welcome " front ; he would not even let them have water with which to make tea—not, at least, till urgent representations had been put over by the troop officer.

The farmer also thought that the arrival of the troops would bring bombing. It was pointed out to him that, if he happened to be right, he would probably need the help of the very men he was antagonising, and, grudgingly, he saw sense.

During that very severe winter of Christmas, 1940, there was a long period during which it was impossible to get fresh rations to the snowed-up troops. They had to make do on iron rations. But, thanks to a good troop officer they didn't miss one mail. Through blizzards, rain-storms, snow, sleet and hail he rode his motor-cycle to and from headquarters, some 30 miles away. Being an officer under these conditions is an arduous, unglamorous job, but a tremendously valuable one. His personality and conduct can make all the difference between philosophical endurance and discontent.

The first winter was not easy. Snow fell early in December, and about Christmas time a frost set in which held until well into February. All over the country there was great inconvenience. To give a typical example, a dozen men at a Light A.A. site in the Basingstoke area were isolated for three days. The ration truck could not get to them nor could the mobile water unit, and it is extraordinary how much snow you have to melt to get enough water for shaving. Over in Norfolk there were gales which drove the snow into drifts, sometimes 15 feet deep. The ration trucks found themselves driving across fields—not that it made much difference where they drove, since there was no prospect of reaching their destinations. Wooden boxes were collected and runners made for them, partly out of bits of old pram, partly with bent steel. The rations were loaded on and pulled three or four miles across fields. Coal was carried in sandbags.

Not even the weather could hold up necessary movements of

units, such as the sending of special protection to areas which might be in special danger. Here is an idea of what conditions on one such move were like, taken from an officer's diary.

" 10th January, 1940. These damn guns were wallowing all over the place. I stood up the entire day, looking backward at the convoy mostly, sometimes looking forwards, but usually with my heart in my mouth wondering how long it would be till something happened. We got to our destination at 18.30 hours. I gave some of the men a rum ration. Riding on top of open vehicles the cold was beyond belief, it would have gone through anything. On the way we passed hundreds and hundreds of duck, mostly teal and mallard, all over the road and railway line ; we really had a difficult time to get them out of the way—poor brutes, I suppose it was cold and hunger. Physically I like to think I am fairly hard—I have been cold before, and hellish cold too, but never in my life have I met anything like this. When we stopped it was difficult to stand, so we were glad to push on, contact with the ice seemed more remote when we were moving."

5. What the Guns Really Do

IN THE first two years of the war, as already stated, A.A. guns were responsible for destroying nearly 600 enemy aircraft over this country. Many more were damaged by A.A. fire, and of these a fair proportion failed to reach their home bases. This is not purely conjecture, but inference from a number of factors, such as the condition of damaged aircraft when last seen and the examination of wreckage and bodies washed ashore.

But the principal achievements of A.A. guns—and this is not generally realised—lie not in the destruction of enemy aircraft, in which their successes, though substantial, are bound to be few compared with the successes of fighter aircraft. The value of the guns is in the prevention of accurate bombing and in preventing enemy aircraft reaching their objectives, particularly by night. The effect of A.A. gunfire is generally speaking, to keep all enemy aircraft at a high altitude and to deter them from flying on the straight and even course necessary for accurate bombing. If a 'plane cannot fly low or straight, it cannot bomb accurately and its chances of doing serious damage are less. Moreover, on many occasions when A.A.

guns have been heavily in action by night, particularly in the London area, 50 per cent. or more of the enemy raiders have turned back before entering the defended area, and many of the raiders which have ventured to enter it have turned back almost at once.

The direct destruction of enemy aircraft is the most obvious purpose of anti-aircraft guns, but this job is much easier for the fighters. For, to bring about the destruction of a 'plane with anti-aircraft fire, the shell must burst within 50 to 100 feet from the target. With light anti-aircraft guns you must hit either the pilot, the engine or the control ; and the fact that an aircraft can suffer a surprising amount of damage in other parts of its structure without being put out of action has been proved by the experiences of our own pilots in action over enemy territory. Even if the shot is perfectly aimed and the fuse is accurately set to burst the shell at exactly the right place and moment, the aircraft only has to deviate from its course to a small extent to escape unharmed.

On the other hand, unless he is using dive-bombing methods, the pilot must fly on a straight and even course at a constant speed for at least half a minute if he is to drop his bombs accurately. When the aircraft is being engaged by anti-aircraft guns the pilot has to decide whether to continue to fly straight, in which case he runs a serious risk of being hit. If, on the other hand, he " jinks " and takes avoiding action by altering his course and speed, then he ruins his bomb-aimer's chance of releasing his bombs accurately.

Another important function of A.A. guns is to indicate the position of enemy aircraft to our own fighters. Often, when an enemy 'plane is out of range, the guns fire one or two rounds to burst as near as possible, simply to draw the fighter's attention to the enemy.

In the nature of things, guns are bound to play second fiddle to the fighters. They have to perform the relatively humdrum job of breaking up large formations of enemy bombers so that the fighters can get in among them, and then put up with the frustration of not being allowed to fire because our own fighters are overhead.

A.A. work is team-work in the highest sense of the word. The wing-forwards, who are the A.A. guns, do their job if they manœuvre the ball into the right place for the centre-forward—the fighter aircraft—to kick a goal.

Guns and gun positions

There are two main types of heavy A.A. gun. The 4.5 inch, which hurls a high explosive shell weighing nearly half a hundredweight to a height of eight miles in 50 seconds' time ; and the

3.7 inch, which has almost as high a ceiling and a faster rate of fire, but a smaller shell. There are also some 3-inch guns from the last war, whose chief characteristic is a high rate of fire ; these fire high explosive or shrapnel shell every three seconds, producing a mushroom growth of cotton-wool bursts.

Our light A.A. gun is the Bofors, which weighs two tons and fires anything up to 120 two-pound shells a minute to a height of 6,000 feet. The shell bursts on impact.

The last-war Lewis gun has been surprisingly successful, mounted singly, or in twin or quadruple for greater fire power. It has brought down many low-flying raiders who sought by diving from cloud to surprise the defences. The function of the light guns is to hold off the bomber from low-level attack, or from vulnerable points all over the country.

At a " heavy " site there may be two, four, six or eight guns. The normal plan is a four-gun site run by a half-battery divided into two sections. The two sites may be several miles from each other.

Suppose a site has been chosen for a new gun position. A point in the middle has been selected from which measurements can be taken to provide accurate data for the guns and instruments when they arrive. This point is indicated, perhaps, by a cross marked on wood bedded in concrete : it becomes the pivot of the gun-site later on. The distance and bearing from this cross to some prominent landmark is established with great accuracy by surveyors and the information is ready for the new Battery when it arrives. Other things are waiting for the Battery, too : a water-supply, which may quite likely consist of one pipe with a tap ; a semi-permanent hut for the Battery office—or it may only be a marquee ; some kind of shed for the cook-house ; and tents or huts for messing and sleeping. There will also be a way into the site—perhaps railway sleepers thrown across a ditch at a point where a gap has been made in the hedge.

These may be the only obvious signs of preparation visible to the new Battery when it arrives ; but, in fact, the selection of the site itself has involved a good deal of work. The reconnaissance of sites is a job in itself ; its principles apply equally to a permanent site, such as the one that is being described, or to a position occupied temporarily by a mobile Battery. In an action of rapid movement A.A. defences must constantly be shifted ; and in choosing successive positions a mobile Battery must apply, so far as it can, general principles. A gun position should, if possible, have an all-round field of fire with no obstruction higher than 10 degrees above ground level.   If, for example, one boundary of the site is screened by tall trees, it would be impossible to see a hostile plane approaching from that direction until it was almost on top of the guns.   The gun position should also allow for effective ground defence : machine-gun posts in particular will have to be chosen to defend the gun site should it be attacked from any quarter.   There must be suitable approaches and exits.   It may be necessary to remove guns at a moment's notice, and if towing vehicles cannot approach easily much time will be lost.   Precautions will have to be taken against sabotage.   Level ground is needed for the guns to stand on. Administrative conveniences have to be considered—proximity of water, telephone, electricity services.   There should be as much cover as possible to make the site inconspicuous from the air ; the ideal gun position will permit the disposition of living quarters, whether tents or huts, in such a way that they do not draw attention to themselves.

When the convoy arrives the Gunners see nothing but a lonely field with a few huts or tents clinging to the hedge-side.   Kit is unloaded, men are detailed to their living quarters, and there is a vague promise of food as soon as the trench fire will boil the dixies.

By next morning the Battery discovers that it can eat, sleep, wash and survive even though it has been plonked down in the middle of a field '' miles from anywhere ''—that is to say about a mile from the nearest bus stop.   And in an extraordinarily short time recon-naissance parties will have thrust round the district and come back to camp reporting amenities within striking distance.

The site has to be improved at once : tracks must be made, as inconspicuous as possible ; rubble and stores unloaded ; and, most important of all, the gun position has to be laid out, for the guns and instruments may arrive at any moment and the first, most urgent duty, is to report the guns '' ready for action '' in the shortest possible time after they arrive at the site.   Among the preliminary activities are the setting up of a shelter cf some sort at the gun position to accommodate personnel who will have to man the operational telephones and plotting devices.   It will also be neces-sary to lay the operational lines from the point where the Signals have brought them to the point chosen for the shelter : this shelter is, perhaps, a tent, which later will be replaced by a hut, and in time by a sunken concrete cabin.

The guns are spaced around the sides of the gun park, with the command post at the centre.   The command post is an oblong enclosure containing the predictor, the identification (or spotters') telescope, and the height-finder.   It is in the charge of the Gun

Position Officer (G.P.O.) who controls the firing of the guns, watches the effect of fire, and has the responsibility of identifying any doubtful 'planes that may be about. He has an assistant—usually an N.C.O., hereinafter referred to as G.P.O.A.—who acts as a human megaphone, relaying the G.P.O.'s orders to the guns : in action the G.P.O.A. is responsible for " fire discipline," for seeing that the correct drill is followed and no unnecessary risks are run. Well-given orders make an extraordinary difference to the number of rounds the guns manage to fire.

Hostile aircraft approaching

An approaching 'plane is first seen through the spotter's telescope, a simple affair with two eye-pieces, which looks quite unlike a telescope. If it is a friendly 'plane, the spotter logs it in a book ; if it is hostile, he sounds the alarm. The trouble starts when he mis-identifies a hostile 'plane as friendly. But spotters are uncannily skilled and their appropriate senses are inhumanly specialised. They are not usually enthusiastic to take on the job, but they quickly develop the specialist's sense of superiority and supplement their official handbooks with privately purchased text-books.

Once the spotter is on the target the G.P.O.A. shouts to everybody else the height and bearing which he reads from scales at the base of the telescope. To do this he must stoop, and, unless he is nimble, he may block the spotter's view. Then the spotter roars out, " Telescope ! Telescope ! " and the G.P.O.A. tries to dodge out of the way without losing sight of the height and bearing scales. For it is not enough to announce where the 'plane was when first seen. The spotter has to keep his telescope on the target as it moves, and, in order to overcome the time-lag between shouting out heights and bearings, and the flight of the 'plane, the G.P.O.A. must estimate ahead : when he is skilful he does not read out the height and bearing registered on the scales, but makes adjustments so that when the predictor and height-finder are registering the figures he shouts, the target will be within their field of view. It is a breathless and exciting business. The G.P.O.A.'s voice is relentless :

" Bearing 154 ! Angle 20 ! " (" Angle " means " angle of elevation ".)

" Bearing 158 ! Angle 20 ! "

Then comes the report :

" Predictor on target ! "

" Height-finder on target ! "

When the G.P.O.A. has heard both these reports, and not before, he tells the G.P.O., " Section on target," and the Battery is ready to make the best use of any information which the predictor may provide.

The heart of the command post is the predictor—the calculating machine that finds out where a 'plane is and predicts its future movements, so that allowances can be made in laying aim. Its calculations are based on information provided partly by the layers and partly by the height-finder, which can tell not only the height of the 'plane but its distance from the gun site.

The findings of the predictor are transmitted to the guns by pointers on dials—two dials for each gun, one recording bearing and one elevation. Gunners, who watch these dials, follow the pointer with another pointer, and by this means swing the gun round and move it up or down according to the readings from the predictor.

In addition to all this activity on ground level, much is done in a shelter probably sunk some way in the ground. This room is the link which every gun position has with the vast system of the Royal Observer Corps and other sources of information. The connection is not, of course, direct ; but the operational line from a central control room in the gun defence area supplies news of the movement of aircraft which is often gathered in the first place from the Royal Observer Corps.

Two telephonists write down and transmit messages between the command post and the gun operations room. This is a trying job, with long hours when nothing is happening : then a lot begins to happen at once ; and if one miscounts the pips it means a wrong plot being made, and perhaps a target being missed.

The G.P.O. and G.P.O.A., standing in the Command Post, can see into the gun-pits. This, too, is essential, because the men in charge of the various gun detachments—the " Numbers 1 "—must acknowledge all orders from the Command Post. By day they shoot an arm straight up ; by night, they use the word "Through! " The importance of acknowledgment cannot be fully realised except during the height of an action, when the noise is deafening and the gun detachments have only one thought—to send up more rounds.

As a rule, each detachment has its own gun which it tends and cherishes with personal affection : this is not surprising, for the gun itself is a graceful and lovely instrument. Perhaps that is why gun crews nearly always give their guns feminine names. This personal affection owes something to the fact that the crews have to build the pit for their gun, and have much the same anxious pride in the task as the dresser of a famous or aspiring actress has in getting her charge ready for a sensational part.

This is how the gunners " make up " their gun. The gun arrives and is levelled. Round it the pit is dug with its half a dozen recesses. The walls gradually rise and are camouflaged, strengthened with sandbags and covered with turf. The recesses are used partly for the storage of ammunition. This has to be stacked with great care. Long, metal boxes, each containing two rounds of ammunition, are stored in such a way that air can circulate all round : no two boxes should touch. Strips of wood separate the layers of ammunition boxes. All the rounds are regularly examined every day to guard against damage by rust or condensation.

One recess is reserved for the Limber Gunner. There should be a strong wooden bench in it so that he can dismantle and clean the breech mechanism. Another recess is used as a shelter. During long night alerts there are many periods when the men cannot leave the gun park, but there is no need for them to be at their positions on the gun. They go to their shelter and sit there in the darkness huddled together and half dozing, but with an ear cocked for " Take Post " ; and when the order comes from the Command Post they have to be back at their positions on the gun in a matter of seconds.

Gunners at play

Normally a gunner has one day off per week and one evening. Why is there so little time to spare ?

There are only two guns per section and only eleven men are needed for each gun team. But apart from the fact, which the outside world finds so difficult to grasp, that when you say you have such and such a number of men on the strength you don't really mean it because most of them are always doing something else, there are various other commitments to be considered.

Take the case of a half-battery, with a nominal roll of, say, 140 men. Ready for action at any minute of every day and night you must have 44 men for the four guns. There must be six to eight men working the predictor and three or four the height-finder. There is a fire picquet, a decontamination squad, stretcher-bearers, a medical orderly and a guard. Five men are away on courses at divisional and brigade schools. Six are away from camp guarding a temporarily unoccupied gun site five miles away. One of the cooks has been commandeered by brigade headquarters. Six men are in hospital and six are sick in camp. Fifteen men are on seven days' leave. Twenty men are having their weekly day off.

That is why only eleven men can go out this evening.

Incidentally, while they are manning the guns or acting as fire picquet, they are kept busy all day with training, with maintenance of their equipment, with P.T., with arms drill, and above all with fatigues and construction work on the camp. There is plenty to do in keeping them up to scratch in all their obligations and duties. For, without the incentive of enemy 'planes to shoot at, efficiency is liable to decline quickly. There is always plenty to do except when it rains.

But it is not a life of all work and no play. Here is a scene which often occurs in every fixed station.

The battery canteen has been transformed into a concert hall. A stage has been rigged up at one end with some rather insecure-looking curtains. The officers sit on chairs in the first few rows ; the men are packed crouch-backed on forms behind. An orchestra of seven is packed at the foot of the stage. Its members keep disappearing, for they provide the bulk of the stage show.

At the moment, the battery sergeant-major and the battery quarter-master-sergeant are doing a cross-talk act which is supposed to be a scene between a sergeant and a new recruit.

What's your trade in civilian life ?

Spotter, chum.

Don't call me chum. Call me sergeant.

What ! Don't you like being called chum, chum ?

Right, we'll try a bit of rifle drill. Now what we're going on with this morning is slope arms by numbers. Slope arms by numbers—one. That's good. Two. Three. Why, you've been in the army before.

No, never, sergeant.

Well, where did you learn that rifle drill ?

I was three years in the chorus of *Desert Song*.

All these shows tend to fall into a generic shape, based on a rather gangling orchestra of about six—piano, drums, piano accordion, saxophone, guitar, possibly a trumpet and a violin. The leader is probably a professional or semi-professional musician of good or fair ability, whose energy is responsible for the organisation of the band. They are almost bound to play " Tiger Rag."

There is likely to be a male voice choir whose choice of music is often strange, ranging from little-known highbrow works to " Oh, who will o'er the Downs so free."

The solo violinist, another fundamental, is more handicapped than the baritone and the tenor by the faulty tuning of the piano. There is the man who does animal impressions, and the man who impersonates Lionel Barrymore and Ned Sparks. There is an occasional freak act. One man eats two lamp bulbs, an ash tray, four safety razor blades and a gramophone record, finishing up with a few lighted cigarettes—all with apparent relish and no ill-effects.

Somewhere in the Command there is a professional escapologist—a fine act.   But good " freaks " are as rare as the piano accordionist is common.   The piano accordionist is the backbone of most concert parties ; his appeal never fails.

Besides the Battery concert parties there are officially constituted and recognised Brigade Concert Parties, such as " The Blue Pencils " and " The Moon and Stars," who do a full-time job and make substantial sums for Army Welfare and regimental funds.   Some Regimental Commanding Officers have formed small concert parties which tour the sites, usually on a part-time basis.   These little concert parties do a lot of good, penetrating where nothing much else does.

Concert parties are officially encouraged by A.A. Command, which has a hierarchy of entertainment officers whose job consists largely in getting things going.   Most officers realise the value of entertainment, especially good home-made entertainment, as an ingredient of morale : but there are a few commanders who believe that entertainment is either unnecessary or actively detrimental : though, in fact, far from taking men's minds off their job, it freshens them by its contrast value.

In addition to these concert parties there is the wireless—notably the special programme broadcast twice a week and known as "Ack-Ack, Beer-Beer," edited by Bill McLurg.   Usually about 40 men and women take part in the programme ; 50 per cent of the actual entertainers are professional or semi-professional in civilian life.

6. The Elephant's Children :

Searchlights in Action

IN ONE OF Kipling's *Just So Stories* there is an attractive character called " The Elephant's Child," whose chief characteristic is " 'satiable curtiosity."   That describes also the chief function of the searchlights.   They probe and swing about the heavens like phosphorescent trunks, seeking the fruit of enemy aircraft in the stellar jungle.   Sometimes they have to operate from sites similar to that favoured by the Elephant's Child which, it will be remembered, was " the great, grey, green, greasy Limpopo River, all set about with fever trees."   So, for example, the Humber may well have appeared to the searchlight crews on the two famous barges, the *Humph* and the *Clem*, stationed there early in 1941, or the Mersey to the crews who reached a certain site on the banks of that river just in time for the blitz of May 1940. Their story is typical of the hot corners in which so many searchlights found themselves, and may be told here.

On May 1st, three nights after their arrival from Orkney, the sirens went just as the clock on Liver Buildings said " ten." The raid lasted for some six hours, but the real ordeal began on the next night. Incendiaries which rained down set fire to piles of timber lying about. The only sand-bags available were on the projector pit. The projector pit came down a lot faster than it had been built.

The following night more than a hundred incendiaries fell on the site, setting fire to the living hut and cook-house. The cook, who was preparing a drop of soup, only knew that two of them came through the roof, and one dropped slap into the dixie of soup. Unfortunately, six of the incendiaries fell inside the projector pit ; one struck the No. 4, putting him into hospital for a month. Those fires had to be put out, and all the men were brought almost to a state of collapse by the heat : the site was a shambles.

They endured this for three more nights until two H.Es. fell on the site, one almost on the generator, the other making a mess of the badly battered sleeping hut.

They had to wait nearly six months for their revenge. On the night of November 1st a Junkers 88 flew over them at 200 feet. He stopped the best part of 86 rounds from their Lewis gun, for which they were given a Category III (damaged) " bird."

In earlier days there was little of such excitement. In the first winter of the war, the Searchlight men were stationed in small detachments on single-light sites. Public appreciation of their work was confined to criticising them when they exposed their lights, on the grounds that they were liable to attract enemy attention. The single-light system did not work very well and was replaced by clusters of three. Having by the end of the first winter made single-light sites fairly habitable, the crews therefore had to re-group themselves on sites built for 10 men, and make them hold about 60. The result was that a large proportion were still under canvas for the second winter of the war. A large number were still under canvas for the third winter when the system had to be changed again back to single-light sites.

Here is a little human story told by a gunner in a searchlight detachment which had just been moved to the middle of a moor. " At last my longed-for night-off arrived. I shaved for the second time, put on my best battle dress, the trousers of which had been under my palliasse for days, and set off to sample a little night life once more. Now, apart from the troop officer's and battery commander's visit, we had seen no one during the three or four days we had been there, and our knowledge of local topography, with special reference to houses of refreshment, was vague. Knowing that I had come in a northerly direction on deployment from civilisation, I reasoned that if I walked south I should find civilisation again, and catch a bus. After 45 minutes' brisk walking without a sign of life, I came across a man trimming a hedge. I happily enquired (*a*) the whereabouts of the nearest town, (*b*) of the nearest pub, and (*c*) what time the last bus went. And received the following astounding replies, (*a*) 12 miles, (*b*) 6 miles, (*c*) Wednesday.''

Of course these discomforts are trivial enough compared to life in a submarine or fighting in the western desert. But when you are concerned in high drama, when your life is in balance, when all your qualities are challenged by vital events, it is easier to give your best. But when, as in the winter of 1939, men were cooped up on searchlight sites without leaving them once for months at a time, without even an afternoon off at the pictures, it was not much wonder that they began to get on each other's nerves. Quarrels would spring up about trivial things—who let the stove out, who left the door open, who took my torch.

Helping the night-fighters

Why was this life necessary ? What was the plan behind it ? In the good old days before the war it was supposed that attacks would be carried out by day and that it would not be possible to bomb effectively in the dark. If night bombing were attempted, the searchlights would provide a six-beam illumination for the guns. The bomber would not be ungentlemanly enough to get out of it, and the gunners would lay their predictor on him, balance it and shoot him down.

One or two people foresaw that London might be effectively attacked at night, that night bombers might not always be illuminated and might not keep the rules laid down for them if they were. For the first nine months there were few targets at all, and daylight shooting misled many people into thinking that the night bomber was not a menace to be worried about.

In the early months if an aircraft changed direction it would be 30 seconds or so before the people on the ground would know that it had done so : and they did not know whether it had gone up or down, or right or left. By the time they had realised that it had changed its direction, it might be anything up to two miles away

On Target ! A 3·7 gun detachment at battle practice. In the foreground, two gunners adjust bearing and elevation as transmitted by the predictor. The Sergeant, back to camera, is ready to give the signal to fire.

A heavy battery of 4·5's in the London area. Gun sites are desolate places; the life of the gunners is lonely and monotonous.

The machine that calculates. Range-finder on a heavy-gun site.

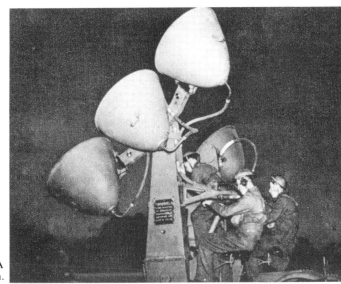

The ears that listen. A sound-locator in action.

" Elephant's Child." A searchlight of 210,000,000 candle-power probes the night sky with its beam.

from where they thought it was. That is why searchlights used to wave apparently aimlessly about in the skies. They were looking on an arc which would bring them across the path of the aircraft whichever way he had turned. It was very confusing to our fighters and they disliked it intensely. We have changed all that now.

Searchlights are now able to help the night-fighters. They indicate to them the present position and course of the enemy aircraft. Incidentally, it is not uncommon for an aircraft to be illuminated as seen by the fighter pilot while from the ground it is invisible.

Searchlights are exposed under the orders of Fighter Command or their lower formation headquarters, in order to make sure that co-operation is perfect.

Lead, Kindly Light

There are other, less commonly known, jobs done by searchlights. They expose their lights to direct home our own aircraft which are lost. As many as 30 aircraft and more have been successfully " homed " in a single night. These incidents run to pattern rather as follows.

It was raining and misty when Gunner Laurence Smith, aged 28, turned out at 5.15 a.m. for duty. Smith, a grocery shop manager until a year before, was still rather sleepy when, nearly two hours later, he heard the faint drone of a British bomber. The clouds were low, the drizzle had given way to heavy storm. As Gunner Smith listened, he detected that the bomber's engines were not running well and guessed that the pilot had lost his way although he was only ten miles from his base. When the bomber came low, Gunner Smith put a beam on it, then flashed the beam across to the bomber's base. He repeated that manœuvre several times until the pilot realised he was being shown the way home. The pilot took the tip, followed the beam across country and landed safely. Another bomber which was also lost followed him in. Not long afterwards messages were sent out asking for the name of the man who had shown such initiative in putting on the beam during daylight. Pilots and crews of both bombers wanted to say " thank you " to Gunner Smith for acting as their guide and probably saving them and the machines.

The searchlights watch the sea. If a man bales out over the Channel there is a most complete system of communication, and intelligence can be passed in a matter of minutes right round to Fighter Command and back again to the rescue parties. If a pilot is seen baling out the word goes round and the rescue launch is sent off at once. It is very much quicker than if it had to be done by local police, who must send their reports through the telephone exchanges.

On one occasion four airmen were reported to be some miles out at sea in a dinghy after their bomber had crashed, but their actual position was not known. The searchlights played on the sea and a Bombardier in charge of the searchlights was the first to sight the dinghy. It was about two miles away. It was held in the light and at first seemed to be drifting towards the shore, but the men were huddled together and in danger of being swamped. A heavy sea was running and it was obvious that the rescue would take some time. But, guided by the light, rescue craft headed towards the dinghy, and at last a corvette steamed into the beam. The four airmen were then picked up and returned to a base.

In a similar way, searchlights in the neighbourhood of balloon barrages must be prepared at any time to illuminate balloons if it appears that our own aircraft are in danger of flying into them. This danger frequently occurs and has frequently been averted.

Searchlight sites are equipped with light machine guns for action against low-flying aircraft. They have shot down many enemy planes. Here is a personal account by L-Bombardier Hanson who shot down a plane on May 10th, 1941.

" Just after midnight we exposed the beam and a few minutes later a 'plane swooped out of the clouds. It was flying very low . . . it couldn't have been much more than 100 feet . . . and we saw at once that it was a Jerry. The Sergeant in charge immediately ordered us to disperse the beam (that's to dazzle the pilot) and ordered machine-gun action. I'd been waiting for that moment for fifteen weary months . . . and I was almost petrified at my luck. The Heinkel didn't seem to be in any difficulties, and as I opened fire I couldn't help wondering why he didn't have a go at us, either with a bomb or a machine gun. After a few rounds the Lewis gun jammed, but we put that right and blazed away again. Then Jerry flew away and we instantly had to engage two more targets with the beam. Ten minutes later, when we'd practically forgotten him, the Heinkel flew back and circled over the site like a giant bat. I didn't have time to think . . . all I remember saying to myself is ' Well, I've been wanting action. Lad, you're going to have a basinful now.' I blazed away and every rifle on the site was being fired in support. After two or three minutes the Heinkel flew away again, but five minutes later it was back for the third time.

" By the fourth time we were getting a bit irritated. The Jerry 'plane was like a mosquito at a picnic. You just couldn't brush the darned thing away.   But this time was K.O.   The 'plane crashed in a nearby field and burst into flames as it hit the ground.   A party was detailed to go to the 'plane and there we found three of the crew dead.   The pilot, who had a machine-gun bullet in his head, wore the Iron Cross.   The fourth member of the crew—I think he was a wireless operator—was staggering about with a bullet in his leg and was obviously dazed and in great pain.   Yes, it was a swell night.   The only fellow who was a bit glum about the whole affair was my mate, whose night off it was.   If it had been the next night, he'd have landed the Jerry instead of me.''

Searchlights also mark the mines which fall in the Thames and other places.   They mark them scientifically by taking the bearing. This, of course, speeds the minesweepers' work and to a certain extent reduces their risks.   It saves a lot of time and a number of ships.

7. The Wonderful Visit

I T   W A S   a fine evening with a dull sky to the north.   About 10.30 p.m. the traces of two unidentified aircraft were picked up by a gun operations room in east Scotland.   They were plotted as approaching the coast from the south of the Faroe Islands.   As they neared land they separated, one turning north and the other continuing overland in a westerly direction.   The 'plane which turned north was soon identified as a friendly one.   The other was presumably hostile.

The raider was again plotted flying due west to the south of Moffat at a height of 5,000 feet, and again south of Cambuslang.   Then the plotting stopped near Busby and all trace was lost.

All gun and searchlight sites were standing by, for the 'plane was getting dangerously near Glasgow.   At 11 p.m. the spotter on a searchlight site about eight miles south of the city saw a 'plane clearly in the moonlight.   He immediately identified it as a Me.110.   The warning was flashed to the heavy guns at Glasgow.   On every searchlight site the Lewis gunner gripped his butt a little tighter in the hope that he might get in a burst at the enemy.

At 11.7 p.m. a neighbouring site again caught a glimpse of the 'plane still flying west.   As they watched, it turned and began to circle the site.   The pilot seemed to be checking his position. Twice it circled round the site.   The air was quiet, the pilot had switched off his engine : and then, to everybody's consternation, he took a shallow dive straight at the site. From the 'plane a parachute streamed out. Some thought, with subsequently growing conviction, that they had seen a man silhouetted against the moonlight as he baled out. Others thought they were being dive-bombed. All thought their last moment had come, but just when the 'plane was about to strike the site it turned off, crashed to the ground not 250 yards away and burst into flames. This was the telephonist's great moment. He proudly reported the affair to headquarters while the detachment formed two parties, one to attend to the burning 'plane, the other to hunt the parachutist.

Meanwhile, two A.A. signalmen, hearing the crashing 'plane, had come running out of their quarters in time to see the pilot floating slowly to earth. Half-dressed, they rushed towards the place where they knew there was a small farmhouse. When they reached it, the back door opened and a ploughman appeared.

" Are you looking for a parachutist ? " he inquired.

They said they were.

" Well, he's inside now, arrived about half a minute ago," said the ploughman.

They dashed into the cottage.

There in an armchair, dressed in a fleece-lined brown leather flying suit, sat the parachutist. He threw out his hands to prove they were empty, and said, " Ah ! British soldiers—no guns—no bombs." They immediately searched him for weapons, but found none. The prisoner also said that his 'plane was unarmed. They asked his name. " Alfred Horn," he replied ; and as they couldn't understand him properly he wrote it down on a piece of paper.

" Where have you come from ? " they asked him. He replied, " Munich in four hours."

One of the soldiers went to telephone headquarters for a car to remove " Alfred Horn," whose ankle was apparently injured by his fall. The other soldier looked curiously at the prisoner, for he had heard much about the poor quality of German clothes. There was nothing of this in the clothing " Horn " wore. His fleece-lined suit and boots were of good leather. He wore a gold wrist watch, and carried what looked like a Leica camera round his neck. A map with his course roughly plotted was strapped round his knee.

He asked if he might keep his parachute as a souvenir. The soldier gave a non-committal reply and asked him if he had ever been to England before. " No," he replied ; and after a pause, " I have a very important message for the Duke of Hamilton," whom he said he had met at the Berlin Olympic Games. He seemed to want to be friendly, and showed them a picture of his wife and son with whom he said he had spent that morning.   One of the soldiers asked him if he would like to return to Germany if he got the chance. He immediately shouted, " No ! No ! No ! No ! "

The scene where the 'plane had crashed was increasingly confused. There were policemen, the Fire Brigade, the A.F.S., the Home Guard, soldiers from neighbouring units, R.A.F. men and many civilians.   The searchlight detachment were ordered to fix bayonets, and even then had great difficulty in clearing the field.   Many pieces of the 'plane had disappeared into the cars in which spectators had arrived, but these were eventually all recovered and handed over.   Its machine guns were brand new.   There was no ammunition, and the gun barrels were filled up with grease.

One of the gunners, on return from escorting the prisoner, had a strong idea that he had seen a photograph of him recently.   Every newspaper and magazine to hand were diligently scanned, and suddenly the gunner shouted, " That's him ! I'm sure that's him ! " He pointed to a photograph of a dark, strongly built man, a Nazi, with thick black hair and deep-set eyes.   It was a photograph of Rudolf Hess, Hitler's Deputy.   How they all laughed.

Their troop officer had been sent to the Home Guard headquarters, where an R.A.F. Intelligence Officer was interrogating the prisoner, assisted by a crowd of officers and others.   The contents of the prisoner's pockets were emptied out on to the desk, including two hypodermic syringes, a phial of liquid and two bottles of white tablets.   The troop officer turned to the R.A.F. officer who was at the moment doing the interrogating, and said :

" You know, sir, I believe this is Rudolf Hess.   I've seen him in Germany, and I recognise him as Hess."

" Don't be a fool," he was told.

He wasn't being.

8. The Blitzes on the Humber

NOW FOR an account in perspective of events and results in a typical area.   It should be emphasised that the only reason why Hull was chosen for this analysis is that it is as good an area as any other.   There are plenty of areas which would have suited the purpose equally well, and there is no suggestion that the defenders of Hull have worked to any better purpose than people in other parts of the country.

In peace-time Hull ranked as " the Third Port and the Ninth City of the British Isles.'' Add the war activities—sea, air and land—of the Humber area, and it becomes a very likely target for the *Luftwaffe*. Look at its geographical position'and it appears to be a fine training target for learner pilots on their early long-range bombing flights. The result is twofold. The tough Yorkshiremen who live there have had more than their share of raids—say a hundred a year—bombing or merely passing over ; while A.D.G.B. Units on the Humber earn the envy of their neighbours who are less frequently in action.

The bulk of the defence has fallen on Yorkshire H.A.A. Regiments. The Searchlight Regiment, which has provided most of the lighting, and a L.A.A. Regiment of Lincolnshire origin have not been without effect in the defence.

The first three months of the war saw very little enemy activity, the first H.A.A. round fired in anger being appropriately on November 5th, 1939, at a low-flying Dornier which escaped. On November 22nd came the first of many mine-layers ; this one impertinently settled on the water and machine-gunned the coast-defence site before flying home. Mine-laying and rather aimless bombing, occasionally directed at searchlights, started and grew during this winter and the spring of 1940. March saw the first raids on Hull itself, during one of which A.R.P. Headquarters were devastated by a direct hit, but were in action again within half an hour in a new building. The summer and autumn, so full of thrilling work at Dunkirk and in the south of England, provided few day raids, for Hull was out of range of dive bombers or fighter escorts. But there was constant mine-laying, with many small and inept raids inland.

From the A.A. defence point of view it was an interesting time. More and more of their customers were night birds, and as the black-out doping of night-flyers was not universal the Searchlights had a busy and productive time. The number of guns then available, and the methods of using them by night, prevented the heavy A.A. from being a very successful weapon. The R.A.F. fighter was the best killer, and on every suitable night all possible help which A.A. units could give was concentrated on assisting the night-fighters, with eminently satisfactory results. Illuminations and interceptions were frequent, and the percentage of German machines shot down was satisfactorily high. The Searchlights also enabled several enemy 'planes to be shot down by the heavy A.A. guns ; and in addition Searchlight Batteries, especially those in the Spurn and Grimsby area, were of constant value for their speed and accuracy in recognising friend or foe in the sky by day or night, by sight or sound, and reporting them. Any A.A. or R.A.F. Commander will tell you the value of a report which establishes the identity of approaching aircraft.

Searchlight sites were often bombed during this period, but nothing suffered much except crockery, rations and the cook's temper. One attack scored a direct hit on a searchlight in action, the bulk of which was later recognised with difficulty some 80 yards away. No. 4 and No. 5 were in the emplacement and were buried, but miraculously were alive when dug out. The Detachment were shaken up ; but they drew a new searchlight next morning and, with the exception of No. 5 who was in hospital, were engaging raiders again that night. On another site, a bomb wrecked the cookhouse but made an excellent duckpond for the Detachment livestock.

By September the combined action of R.A.F. Fighters and A.A. Units had obviously made this area so dangerous that raiders usually swung well clear to the north or south of the Humber as soon as they had made their landfall. Throughout the autumn this state of affairs continued, German attacks being light apart from mine-laying, and long hours of cold nights were spent trying to manoeuvre evasive Germans into areas where guns or fighters could have at them. On the ground it was a busy time. A new Searchlight policy entailed endless digging, moving huts and training. Heavy A.A. and light A.A. were all but overwhelmed by a huge intake of civilians whom they converted into soldiers without relaxing their operational work. A new method of Fire Control was studied, introduced and developed, and Humber heavy A.A. put much original work into its development. Much was done to assist the Navy in preventing and locating mine-layers. The problem of the blacked-out bomber was constantly with them, for the many raids which have been lightly passed over were each of them a very real anxiety. And so ended 1940, in ice and snow, like its predecessor—and the Humber can be cold. Humber A.A. defences had acted largely as handmaid to the R.A.F. and to the Navy, and as nursemaid in its own establishment. Though the enemy 'planes brought down by the guns were still in single figures, they had helped in many hunts where the actual kill was entered in another game book.

The attacks grow fiercer

With the opening of 1941 the Hun appeared to lose his proper respect for the defences of the Humber, came in closer and dropped more bombs in the area, though often with poor aim. Heavy A.A., light A.A. and Searchlights joined hands and responded to the opportunity. Quoting from the War Diary :—

Night Feb. 9/10 : 15-20 Aircraft.   S.Ls. illuminated eight aircraft some for two minutes.   Two shot down, one by H.A.A. and one by L.A.A., both illuminated throughout engagement.

Night Feb. 10/11 : 30 Aircraft including HE 115 floatplanes.   Several illuminated.   S.L. 05G picked up target, passed it on to S.L. 05H who passed in turn to S.L. 05J.   " RR " L.A.A. site engaged, firing 5 rounds 40 mm. and 340 rounds .303.   Plane shot down into the sea.

Night Feb. 14/15 : 20-30 Aircraft.   Ten illuminations averaging $1\frac{1}{2}$ minutes " RR " L.A.A. site got another—a Ju 88—with 12 rounds 40 mm.

Humber suffers as a " stand " because a gun loses so many of his birds in the water ; but it was a good and exciting time which lasted till losses such as the above, with many others which could not be seen and substantiated, drove the Hun away to do his mine-laying in less expensive areas.   Heavy A.A. shared in the bag but the light A.A. had most of the fun at this time.   One of their Sergeants gave an excellent broadcast on it.

February, March and April were packed with raids, mine-laying raids, raids on Hull and raids on other parts of the area.   On March 22nd a daylight raider, who had lost his way, came out of low clouds over a well-defended area inland.   A hot reception drove him back into the clouds unhurt.   His next descent from the clouds found him in the very centre of the Humber area with Heaven knows how many fingers itching on their triggers.   Light machine-gun fire instantly wrecked both engines and killed the observer.   The pilot just had time to release his bombs before he hit a tree.   Somehow he got out alive.   Everyone claimed this 'plane, but an extremely tough Light A.A. Subaltern got there first and abolished the claim of the Balloon Barrage.   It was eventually allotted to his Troop, though the work may well have been shared by a Lewis Gunner of the Searchlights, who apologised to his Colonel for shooting in front of the target.   All through these months R.A.F. fighters were co-operating as before, but these low flyers were more the guns' meat than theirs.   There is a satisfactory list of enemy 'planes engaged by the R.A.F. with and without A.A. co-operation from January to April.

Blitz attacks had been an anxiety for some time.   A fire control team, sent out from Humber to assist in training other gun zones, had brought back first-hand information from Coventry.   Sheffield, a sister gun-zone, handed on the lessons learnt there.   Continual thought and work had been given to the problem, and May brought full trial to Humber A.A. Defences.   Each night from the 2nd to the 6th saw some activity, and on May 7th and 8th there were really serious attacks lasting between four and five hours. On each night fire bombs fell first and then H.E. was dropped into the fire area.

The first night was a broadcast affair, doing much damage and causing fires here, there and everywhere throughout Hull. The second attack appeared to be far better carried out ; either the fires still burning helped the Germans, or better squadrons were used, or possibly ginger had been distributed for the rather slipshod bombing of the night before. Incendiaries started fires near the centre of the town, and bombing worked steadily eastward parallel with the river, firing stack after stack of timber. High explosives followed accurately in the path of the incendiaries and soon there appeared to be five miles of flame, punctuated by the flashes of bombs, and more encouragingly by those of guns and shells. Early on the first night communications were badly deranged ; but steps taken beforehand enabled an efficient tactical and technical control of guns and searchlights to be maintained throughout both nights.

From the defence point of view results were disappointing on the first night. Nothing had quite worked ; although there were many reports of enemy casualties, few could be substantiated ; but in any case all were too busy putting things right to worry overmuch about claiming casualties. The second night was one of clear cold moonlight, with a red glow and a black pall of smoke over Hull. High-flying Huns left vapour trails which could be seen with the naked eye. If the Hun had improved his technique, so had we ; and with one or two minor hitches our carefully thought-out plans worked. Soon after the attack began, wireless messages were coming through from pilot after pilot of Huns engaged and falling, each checked up a few seconds later by searchlight reports of machines falling in flames. Nor were the guns idle : they shot down only one less than the R.A.F. that night. No third attack came, despite the fires that burnt. Had it come, all was ready to raise the scale of Hun casualties once more. Hull had been hammered but had hit back.

There was an almighty crash

There was much gallantry abroad those two nights, first and foremost among A.R.P. and A.F.S. personnel, who kept damage and casualties down and courage up by their untiring and undismayed work in these as in all other raids. When the first attack began those at '' C '' heavy A.A. site not serving the guns were celebrating a visit of the Brigade Concert Party, followed by a dance. It was a pre-war '' militia '' site, better furnished with huts

than the war-time model.   As the guns opened, the Battery Commander walked towards the Canteen to warn civilian guests that a
raid was on.   A sentry suddenly dashed past him shouting a warning.
Hardly were the words out of his mouth before there was an almighty
crash and half the camp went up.

The first thing the Battery Commander heard as he picked himself
up was the National Anthem being sung in the remains of the
wrecked canteen to end the concert, and the voice of an N.C.O.
turning out and organising the fire picquet.   The camp caught fire
from end to end, and the blaze was far more than local appliances
could cope with.   Armed with axes, crowbars and bare hands,
Officers, Warrant Officers, N.C.Os. and all who could be spared
from the guns, including two prisoners from the Guard Room, broke
into collapsed and blazing huts, dragged out stunned men who had
been trapped there and rendered first aid.   Back came the Hun,
showering incendiaries, but the workers were too busy to notice
them at the time.   Four men were killed and a dozen injured ; but
without the superhuman efforts which seem to have come naturally
to everybody at the time, some 50 or 60 would have died in the
burning camp.   Throughout, the guns of " C " Station continued
their engagement of the enemy.   And the A.T.S. kept making tea.
One is glad to record that on the next night this Station scored a
direct hit on an enemy 'plane which exploded and came down in
fragments.

Down in the Docks a Light A.A. Detachment kept their gun in
action, firing whenever the billowing smoke gave them a chance.
In the intervals they saved their own M.T. and much else from fire
and dealt with incendiaries as these arrived.   Soon a very near miss
severely wounded both M.T. drivers and caused several minor
casualties.   The Subaltern in command handed the gun over to the
Sergeant and drove them through a rain of H.E. and incendiaries,
past or through bomb-holes, negotiating fallen tram and telephone
poles and cables, past shattered and blazing buildings.   He got his
men to hospital, had his own wound dressed, returned to his site
and resumed command.

The good barge *Clem*, which with her sister ship the *Humph*,
mounts searchlight and Lewis gun and leads an exciting life in the
Humber, shot down a raider which came screaming out of the
artillery concentration into the fancied security of the river.

There are many more tales of these two nights—tales of medical
orderlies and drivers, tales of signallers mending cables under fire,
tales of officers, cooks and clerks tripping and sweating in the cold
night to carry ammunition or make recalcitrant guns " run out "

to the firing position. There are tales of gallantry but also of clear heads used with determination.

Small raids continued during May, but were dealt with by the guns and did little damage. June, July and August saw continuous enemy activity in the area and an increasing percentage of enemy machines shot down, chiefly by heavy A.A., but with Bofors and Lewis guns scoring when the chance came to them. Late June and July brought a series of well-executed enemy raids by 35 to 50 'planes each time, which caused considerable damage until an answer was found to the method of attack used. During one of these raids heavy A.A. fire shook up a raider at 10,000 feet ; he lost height rapidly and was picked up by a searchlight south of the river. The enemy dived on the searchlight, dropping incendiaries and high explosives, one of which pitched 50 yards from the site and knocked the Subaltern and Lewis Gunner off their feet. The searchlight held the 'plane, which circled as if to attack again ; but the Subaltern picked himself up, ran to the gun, and his bullets finished the engagement, for the 'plane dived and crashed. After August, Germany's other interests gave Humber its quietest time since the beginning of 1940, but the few Huns who came within range suffered a high percentage of casualties. The bag for 1941 was several times greater than for 1940.

The story ends with a footnote in the first person. " We have done our share of killing, in addition to ' driving ' for the R.A.F. Much of our work is unknown and done in the dark, trying to help Bomber or Fighter in case of need. Signallers work endlessly so that no point in the game be lost ; despatch riders face night, snow, fog and slippery roads so that essential orders of the day reach every site. What I write may seem poor comfort to the people of much-blitzed Hull, yet our close co-operation and good fellowship with the civilian population is of the best. They realise our difficulties and our efforts, and their tough, cheerful, Yorkshire spirit does the rest. We cannot say we have kept the enemy away ; no air or ground defence yet invented can say that, but there are many raiders which have turned away and many bombs which have fallen harmlessly in fields or water. We have done our best to use the men, the resources and the brains available, we have tried never to stand still but to progress, we have shared the dangers and we have hit back. And we are still of the same mind and of the same determination."

These are the men, duplicated all over the British Isles, who made sure that, though the Bomber may " always get through," he does not always get home.

9. The Battle of Britain Begins:
Defending the Airfields

WHEN A HEAVY A.A. gun fires at night there is a flash of flame 25 feet high, and there had never been a published picture of this instant. So it was arranged that an expert Press photographer should take one. Many have been taken since, but this was the first. He went to a gun site guarding Avonmouth and Bristol, which at the time (July 1940) were getting plenty of enemy attention. He focused his camera in daylight, got the four guns in the view-finder and fixed the tripod in position ; he arranged to open his shutter when the gun position officer gave the command " Fuse ! " and then settled down to wait.

It was not a very luxuriously appointed site, and there was only one officer, who slept and ate in his office with a half-bottle of whisky as his mess bar. They slept in their clothes, except the photographer, who ran out in his pyjamas and a tin hat whenever there was an alert, which seemed to be about once in ten minutes. But the enemy, trying for Avonmouth, were always too high for the guns to get a chance to fire. For eight days the photo-grapher waited in the alternate patience and impatience of a photo-grapher after a picture. On the eighth night, at 3 a.m. and in drizzling rain, the alarm was sounded. He rushed to his position, his left hand on the shutter, his right hand holding the camera. The searchlights caught and held the target, like a little silver cigar pendant in the darkness. The gunners went into action, and as their officer shouted " Fuse ! " the photographer opened his shutter and waited. There was an almighty explosion. The four guns had gone off all together, smashing the barrack-hut windows, jerking the camera several feet into the air, cutting the photographer's left cheek and knocking one of his teeth out, shooting the tail off the 'plane and bringing it down.

The photographer, congratulated by an officer on a wonderful picture, moaned in reply that he hadn't got a picture at all. He was very depressed ; he phoned his office and they told him to come home. Just to round off the story, he had to smash up his car on the way back to avoid a suicidally-swerving cyclist.

Of course the story had a happy ending, for when, in a mood of self-torturing determination to pursue this fiasco to its final disap-pointment, he developed the pictures, there emerged the triumphant photograph reproduced between pages 48 and 49.

This picture was taken in July 1940. The Battle of Britain was just starting. The guns were at last going to have a chance to show what they could do.

The Germans started the Battle of Britain with attacks on convoys, and then went on to harbours and dockyards. They bombed Chatham Dockyard. They delivered mass attacks on Portsmouth and Dover ; they bombed Portland and Weymouth ; and then, while still maintaining attacks on coastal towns, started a carefully-planned series of assaults against airfields.

The importance of A.A. guns in airfield defence is fundamental. It is the guns which guard the 'planes during the vital moments when they are getting off the ground. Wherever in this war airfields have lacked adequate A.A. defences, they have been unable to stay in action under any sustained attack. This was amply demonstrated in France and Crete. Nine of the airfields in South and South-east England came in for a battering, some of them twice in one day, and in a few instances airfields were attacked several times during a day.

Here is an example of the quick action and readiness of the anti-aircraft defence on airfields. One afternoon, when a number of our own aircraft were refuelling at a southern airfield, enemy raiders came and had an excellent chance of attacking the personnel and 'planes on the ground. The A.A. guns opened up at the raiders at once, with such success that the enemy could not get in to bomb or machine-gun the ground in spite of determined effort. They jinked and turned to starboard, and unloaded their bombs on a building at the side which had been a hospital, a small part of which was occupied as a military office. The airfield and the 'planes were saved by A.A. fire on that occasion, though the building which received the bombs was set on fire and partially destroyed.

On August 15th, Manston and Hawkinge airfields were dive-bombed by a hundred enemy aircraft which dived out of the sun with engines shut off. The raid split and 50 raiders attacked each place. In the Hawkinge attack a hangar was hit and some damage done to administrative buildings, but the landing ground was not affected. The formations were quickly broken by hot A.A. fire, and the enemy became so anxious to leave the area that his bombers threw away their bombs over Ramsgate and Broadstairs where private property and small civilian homes suffered. Some people were killed but no military casualties or damage resulted. Similarly at Manston airfield the landing ground was untouched ; some damage, however, was done to surrounding buildings.

The next day Tangmere was attacked by 200 Junkers 87s. Then 24 Stukas, flying at 15,000 feet, dived in pairs to 1,200 feet. One of the Bofors brought a 'plane down with only two rounds, the first of which was a direct hit. This gun was firing over open sights. This was Tangmere's most serious raid. Seven R.A.F. personnel and two civilians were killed. But 20 enemy aircraft were brought down and the airfield was in action again within a few hours.

Three days later came another big-scale airfield attack. Kenley and Biggin Hill were among the main targets, and were attacked by raiders numbering 35 to 100 aircraft. Much damage was done. The attack on Kenley was made in two waves. The first was a low-level attack at 1.22 p.m. by nine Dornier 17s, flying as low as 50 feet. These raiders were plotted in the whole way from Newhaven. The searchlight control officer at Kenley said, " We followed the 'planes every inch of their journey, and knew they were making for us." The first three of the low-flying raiders machine-gunned the pits of the 3-inch guns manned by a Light A.A. Regiment and dropped bombs on the northern edge of the airfield. The remaining six raiders dropped high explosives and incendiaries on the Troop H.Q., the Hospital and the Hangars, scoring direct hits. In all 50 or 60 H.E. bombs were dropped.

The high-level attack came from the direction of Dungeness and caused very little damage.

They shook the Luftwaffe's nerve

During their action against the raiders one of the 3-inch guns hit a Dornier square on the nose and brought it down. A Gunner, who was knocked off his perch and wounded by bomb splinters, refused to leave his post. Some of the bombs were dropped from so low a level that they reached the ground still horizontal, and skidded along making grooves before they hit the wall of the Officers' Mess. All the R.A.F. telephone lines were wrecked ; but fortunately the Army Lines to the Searchlight Batteries were unharmed, and over these medical aid was summoned. Lewis Gunners of the L.A.A. Regiment reported that their bullets seemed to glance off the enemy aircraft without having any effect. This was confirmed by the R.A.F. fighters, and was one of the first indications that the *Luftwaffe* were putting heavier armour on their machines. Nevertheless, 29 enemy aircraft were brought down.

At Biggin Hill the story is similar. One hundred 'planes raided Biggin and 200 bombs were dropped. The Heavy and Light guns were in action, the former claiming one Dornier 215. The Bofors No. 2 gun site had a narrow escape. Three anti-personnel bombs were dropped in their compound, two of them missing the magazine only by inches. Splinters from one of these bombs killed the detachment cook, seriously wounded the Troop Commander and slightly wounded one other rank. Skilful plotting by a neighbouring Searchlight Battery saved many aircraft from being destroyed. Their preliminary reports enabled all aircraft, including even trainers, to be got off the ground in time. Finally, the operations room had to be evacuated. The Searchlight Control Officer went back to see that everything was clear and found that the one telephone left intact was ringing. It was a call from the Observer Corps. A voice asked, " Are you interested in a crashed Hurricane ? " Bdr. E. W. Lelliott was praised for his cool leadership and the valuable notes which he took of new tactics used by the enemy 'planes.

The next day, August 19th, raiders were engaged by A.A. guns over the Thames Estuary. About 20 bombers with a large fighter escort appeared at 15,000 feet. The first 'plane to be hit by A.A. fire lost height rapidly and dived away to the south-east, eventually crashing near Faversham. The second salvo hit another plane which crashed at Leysdown, the pilot baling out. The action continued and the formation was broken in a very few minutes. A number took sudden avoiding action and two were seen flying seawards and losing height rapidly.

Towards the end of August it became very noticeable that most of the raiding aircraft approaching these shores took care to avoid areas where they had been so mauled by A.A. fire for the past three weeks. Raiders which came within A.A. guns' range at all took immediate avoiding action from the first shell-burst, or operated from very great heights. Examples of this respect for the guns were the attacks on Chatham Dockyard and the airfields at Eastchurch and West Malling on the night of August 28th. The damage to these targets was negligible and the 'planes flew so high as to be well out of gun range. Though it was impossible for the bombers to get correct aim from such a height, they preferred not to test the A.A. fire ; at 2 a.m., however, one of them did venture down to 13,000 feet above Chatham. He was last seen flying just above the sea with his port engine on fire and little chance indeed of reaching home.

On the last day of August there were further and more determined attacks, which were put to flight by A.A. fire. R.A.F. pilots witnessed a number of hits on the enemy raiders. They were able also to locate individual raiders with the help of bursts from the guns which, though the enemy were a little out of range on several occasions, served as pointers to our fighters to follow up and engage. The next day a single reconnaissance 'plane strayed into range of the guns at about 10.15 p.m., was engaged at once and exploded in the air.

10. The Great London Barrage

THE BATTLE OF BRITAIN was still in full swing when the first night attack was made on London on September 6th/7th, 1940. The daylight battles had begun to go against the Germans, though they were still continuing them.

London at this time was not adequately defended. All over England there was still a shortage of anti-aircraft guns, and as we might be attacked anywhere, it was essential to give cover to all our large cities. In the Thames Estuary a considerable concentration of anti-aircraft guns had been built up, because many of the German daylight attacks were made *via* the Thames Estuary. But now it was essential that the gun defence of London should be rapidly improved. Within 24 hours of the first night attack reinforcements from all over the country were on their way to London, and within 48 hours the guns in London had been doubled.

The initial attacks on London were made on the East End docks and caused very great havoc. It appeared as if the enemy thought that by concentrating on the East End, where there was a large and crowded population, he would cause such panic as to endanger the Government's position, if not to force them to make peace. Thanks to the stubbornness, first of the people in the East End, and later of all Londoners, this indiscriminate bombing of the civilian population did not result in any serious loss of morale. At the same time, the very courage of the Londoner constituted an obligation to defend him.

A.A. guns take a little time to be effective after they have moved into new positions. Telephone lines have to be laid, gun positions levelled and the warning system co-ordinated ; it was, therefore, disappointing that, though the reinforcements in guns by the second night of the battle were very considerable, there did not appear to be much more A.A. fire.

Before the war a very complicated system of barrages, depending primarily on sound locators for their information, had been organised. It was known as the " Fixed Azimuth " system.

Battle of Britain. Vapour trails in the sky, as a hundred enemy aircraft streamed towards London in August, 1940.

Field watching-post. Men of the Royal Observer Corps detect and plot the course of an enemy raider.

Plotting board. At an Observer Corps centre, coloured counters follow the movements of hostile aircraft on a huge plot of the area.

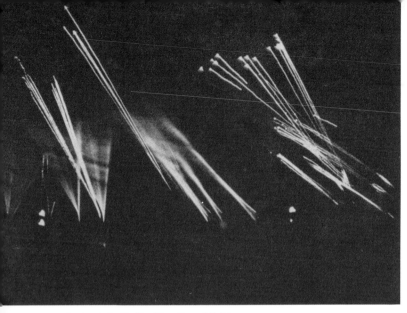

Hitting back at the Luftwaffe. Searchlights
and tracer shells over a South Coast town.

Looking for trouble. Cones of concentrated searchlight beams during a raid on London.

" There was an almighty explosion." The first picture of A.A. fire at night (cf. p. 44). This salvo jerked the camera several feet into the air, knocked out one of the photographer's teeth, and shot off the tail of the enemy aircraft.

Good shooting! A German bomber
brought down in a Midland farmyard.

A Messerschmitt 109 shot down by
Lewis-gun fire in a Kent cornfield.

Special regiments had been trained in its use, and during the early stages of the war it had been improved very greatly. But, depending as it did on sound for its information, it was both inaccurate and cumbersome, and it could only produce a small volume of fire for the large number of guns.

During the nights of September 8th and 9th, Command and Divisional staffs visited gun sites and consulted together in Gun Operations Rooms in order to try and produce a more effective answer to the German night raids. But, though variations of all sorts were put into effect on the night of the 9th with a view to producing greater accuracy, everyone on the Command and Divisional staffs was most dissatisfied with the results. Early on the morning of the 10th, a conference was held at Command headquarters with the determination that, whatever had gone before, on that Wednesday night the enemy should be met with a barrage the like of which had never been seen or heard before. Great difficulties were still encountered. Radiolocation, though it had been progressing marvellously, was still in its infancy, and very few gun positions were equipped even with the radio warning sets. Even sound locators, which were in use with the "Fixed Azimuth" system, were really only capable of giving the height at which the enemy was travelling perhaps ten miles away from the Capital ; on the gun site itself there was no method of finding out whether the height had changed.

After a very earnest consultation with scientists and experts of all sorts a meeting was called in London for 12.30 that day. The Gun Position Officers (*i.e.*, the officers in charge of firing the guns) from every site in London were directed to attend, in addition to the Battery, Brigade and Divisional Commanders. It was made a point of honour with these G.P.Os.—many of them young officers who a few months before had been civilians—that, however handicapped they might be by shortage of equipment, they should put up such a barrage that night as, if it did nothing else, would hearten the civilian population. All the schemes that the scientists could devise were explained to them ; and as a final bit of advice they were told that, where all else failed, they would get a height sent to them from the Gun Operations Room and they must use their ears to estimate where the enemy was, and then barrage in front of them at that height.

" *I never slept so peacefully* "

The result was remarkable. Punctually to time the German bombers arrived—and were met by a roar of guns which must have astonished them as much as it heartened the Londoners.   The enemy had been flying at 1,200 feet ; as soon as the barrage opened they climbed to 22,000 feet.   Many turned back and at least nine 'planes were shot down by A.A. fire.   Guns were in action all night ; and at dawn, as the ammunition lorries moved into the sites to replenish the unprecedented number of rounds which had been fired, the gunners were washing out the hot bores of their guns.

The Regional Commissioner had been warned that there would be a great deal of heavy fire in London that night, so that he could get the wardens in charge of the shelters to explain it.   There was, however, no need for this precaution.   Everywhere in London people said, '' Thank God we are fighting back.''   Though the number of enemy aircraft destroyed that night was not large in proportion to the prodigious number of rounds fired, the morale of London jumped 100 per cent.   The next morning every newspaper came out with emblazoned headlines on London's barrage.

On that barrage, so crudely begun, has been built up the most effective defence that all our scientific brains could produce.   It has, moreover, become a pattern for the defence not only of the cities of Great Britain, but our fortresses abroad and the cities of other mighty adherents to the United Nations.

The best tribute to the barrage from Londoners is the remark heard on every side the next day, '' I never slept so peacefully in my life as when I heard those guns booming ! ''

The Command was so short of men during the winter of 1940-41 that to a certain extent London had to be reinforced with recruits strange to gunnery and unfamiliar with fire discipline.   Take the specimen case of a battery stationed at Cleethorpes, where for many weeks it had kept watch over the Humber without being called upon to fire a round.   It was ordered to London.   Twenty-five hours later the battery was on its new site—a site almost completely unprepared.   Ground, clogged with bricks, mortar and stone, had to be levelled.   Guns had to be laid down, instruments connected up, and supplies of ammunition arranged.   A 3-ton R.A.S.C. lorry was pressed into use as a men's canteen and another as a sergeants' mess.   By 7.30 p.m. all essential work had been done and the guns were ready.

At 8.15 p.m. the alarm was given.   The battery opened with a barrage which had to be worked out on the spot, as ready communication with a central control was not available.   At 6 a.m. the order '' Stand Easy ! '' was given, to the relief of four gun teams of dead-beat men.   But it was only '' Stand Easy ! '' as far as action was concerned.   There was work to be done in boiling out, servicing and polishing the guns. It was 9.30 a.m. before the men went to sleep, in tents, with the bare ground as their bed. Half an hour later came the first of many daylight alarms ; and each time, so near the bare existence-line was that mobile battery, the same men had to take posts. For eight days the procedure was the same. Alarms by day, continuous barraging by night, and so little sleep that at times the layers were almost unconscious as they tried to keep their eyes focused on the dials.

Then the relief came

On the ninth day relief came, in the shape of troops who had done no more than the basic military training that precedes every A.A. man's introduction to gunnery. Only two hours were available in which to instruct them in their duties. The question was how they would react when the enemy was engaged. To be on a gun in action for the first time can be unnerving. Older hands stood near them as they applied bearing and elevation for their first shots in the night battle of London. But after three rounds had been fired the older hands were ordered to fall out.

A battery manning 4.5-inch guns on the Isle of Dogs caught the brunt of the big attack on the London Docks on September 7th. Many of the gunners had been in uniform only a few weeks. In fact, when the first warning came through from Gun Operations Room, Captain Fletcher, the site commander, was inspecting a fresh intake of men who had never before been on a gun position. Their training was to be expedited by events. For three days and nights the action raged. Right at the beginning a heavy bomb landed on the road leading to their guns, ruling out any chance of transport getting through with supplies. Their greatest worry was ammunition replenishment, but the R.A.S.C. lorries arrived regularly and the gunners carried every round a hundred yards over the bomb-torn ground to their gun-pits.

Captain W. J. S. Fletcher was given the immediate award of the M.C. for his courage, leadership and devotion to duty. In the short lulls between actions he went out searching the site and the devastated neighbourhood for unexploded bombs which threatened both men and equipment. Frequently he led parties of gunners to deal with explosive incendiary bombs. There was not a hope of putting out the fires which ringed and lit up the site, but he kept many of them under control.

In those days conditions on gun sites, though better than at the beginning of the war, were still not very good. The majority were deep in mud, and the gunners lived in crude dug-outs immediately beside the gun-pits. Blast from the guns soon told on these quarters. Many of them collapsed, and nearly all of them soon became so badly warped from bomb and gun blast that it was useless attempting to pump out the rain-water.

At one point in the Battle of London the enemy concentrated on gun sites. Although bombing was severe and several sites received either direct or nearby hits, the total casualties were very slight and there was relatively small damage to equipment. Not one battery was put out of action. Seventy-three H.Es. fell within a quarter of a mile of one site ; on another site three heavy bombs exploded over the guns. Barrack huts and stores were destroyed, and in some cases communications were interrupted. On a site in the South-east a bomb landed outside the guard-room, shattering a complete row of huts. Immediately afterwards a Molotov Bread-basket unloaded itself over the camp. Twenty fires flared up ; but the fire picquet, aided by the A.F.S., put them out before much harm had been done.

Der Tag

A week after the London barrages first flowered came the peak of the daylight attacks. Sunday, September 15th was one of our fighter pilots' great days. The enemy attacked with more than 500 'planes, at that time the largest force ever launched in a single day's offensive, and lost at least 185 of them. Here is the anti-aircraft side of the picture.

In the morning attack the guns could play little part because of the presence of friendly fighters, though, of course, they did their usual job in breaking up formations. Their opportunity came in the afternoon. At about 2.30 p.m. the first of two great waves of enemy planes, each more than 150 strong, crossed the coast between Dover and Dungeness, and thrust towards the Thames Estuary. Less than a hundred of them managed to elude the fighter net and reach the south-eastern outskirts of London. Eight minutes after crossing the coast it was apparent that they were headed straight for the Chatham guns. There was not long to wait. Distant thuds came in quick succession as the West Malling guns engaged them. A curtain of white puffs, remote and unreal, shrouded the toy-like specks. One of them fell away trailing black smoke. Now they could be identified through binoculars, about 40 Dornier 215s in close arrowhead formation with their fighters, flying at 18,000 feet and 250 m.p.h.

The staff officers who provided the material for this story were watching from one of the old forts of Chatham, built to repel an earlier invasion which never came. The bombers came steadily on. The range shortened. From the sunlit town there was neither noise nor movement.

Then the outer gun stations went into action. The black bursts of the first salvoes sprang up among the leading bombers. The foremost Dornier swerved and dived away, a long plume of smoke trailing from its cockpit. From the engines of the second came thin wisps of white smoke that grew to a cloud. The formation turned away from the wall of bursts towards the Medway, climbing steadily and spreading widely like the fingers of an outstretched hand. One of them exploded with a direct hit, and a string of flaming fragments fell towards the river. More and more gun stations took up the action : there was an infernal crescendo of sound. For half a minute—how disproportionately short these significant battles are—the Dorniers pressed on in formation. Then, over Dartford, the close wedge was broken, and as the bombers scattered to avoid the bursting shells, Hurricanes and Spitfires, diving out of the sun, did execution.

Meanwhile to the south-west of Chatham a second wave of Heinkels was similarly faltering under intense gun-fire. Long before the Medway was reached its ranks had degenerated into a straggling line, widely dispersed.

For some minutes the cloudy sky above the Isle of Grain was the setting for high drama. The routed Dorniers of the first wave were staggering about in dogfights, the sky a wild medley of twisting aircraft. The white discs of parachutes hung in the air. Over Chatham the guns still held the stage and the Heinkels of the second wave rocked and jinked as they tried to run the gauntlet of the barking inner guns and the cruisers in the river. The leading Heinkel, caught in a salvo of 3.7-inch shells with its bomb-load still in the racks, blew to pieces at 19,000 feet. Almost at the same instant another Heinkel, hit in the cockpit and engines, fell flaming down towards Dartford Park. Thirty seconds later, over the Isle of Sheppey, the guns shot away the tail of a third machine which dived 5,000 feet into the sea and disappeared entirely. The guns had shot down three raiders in less than three minutes.

Not far away the Bofors gunners engaged a Dornier flying fast and low towards the sea. Repeated hits were scored , the target danced antics in the air ; both engines caught fire, and he turned over and fell towards the sea. The air at this time was full of the crumps of bursting salvoes, the whine of falling shell splinters, the uproar of engines. And as the London batteries engaged, the din was multiplied.

A third wave of enemy approached, mainly Dorniers, at slightly over 16,000 feet. This was the last mass-formation attack of the day. It was not a mass formation for long. It was quickly scattered by the guns, and while out of range of the majority of batteries, the enemy turned away westwards to meet the Nemesis of further fighter squadrons.

In the mopping-up actions, when the returning enemy came within range at all, two more Dorniers and a Messerschmitt 109 fell to the heavy guns and two Dorniers to the light A.A. batteries. It is not possible to detail all the incidents of that crowded half-hour which, of course, seemed like hours of battle to the people who took part. A fugitive Dornier appeared out of the clouds over a Bofors position to be shot down in flames only 500 yards from the gun-pit. A Messerschmitt, its tail shot away at 15,000 feet, whined down to shatter itself in a rural churchyard. Another Dornier, already hit in the port engine, blundered over Chatham at 5,000 feet. As the 4.5-inch bursts sprang up beside it, pieces of wing and fuselage broke away from it. Four occupants baled out and were captured by cheering civilians who raced across the fields while the pilotless bomber, skimming the roof-tops, buried itself in a cottage garden.

Shortly before five o'clock the gunners of a cargo vessel steaming down the river hit a Heinkel with their twelve-pounder at 200 yards' range, and saw it crash into the mudflats on the Essex side of the river.

During these late engagements cloud almost completely covered the sky and visibility grew gradually worse. It was under these conditions that the last action of the day took place. At 5.15 p.m. a single Dornier 215 dived from low cloud, cracking away with its machine gun at the streets of an estuary town. At 3,000 feet a Bofors opened up and brought it down flaming—a red exclamation mark to close the story of a memorable day.

11. Portsmouth Fights Back

WE HAVE traced the progress of the German air offensive through its successive stages up to the culminating day. Broadly speaking, whatever type of objective the enemy chose (he switched from one type to another at quite short intervals) he was baffled by a defence in which the gunners played their full part. After his defeat on

September 15th it is possible, perhaps, to detect yet another change in objectives. Instead of attacking categories of things, such as ships, docks or airfields, the enemy tended to attack places, or in the phrase which the Russians have made famous, " inhabited localities," and to attack them by night instead of by day. These concentrated blitzes led to the coining of a new verb, to coventrate, from the spectacular night blitz on Coventry. All such attacks are very similar in character. When one has been described, all have been described. We hope, therefore, that nobody's feelings will be hurt if we select as a specimen one of the so far lesser-known of these attacks, and tell the story of Portsmouth.

The late winter and early spring of 1940-41 had been fairly quiet. After a big raid on Southampton on December 1st there was a tailing-off in enemy activity. By day the *Luftwaffe* concentrated on reconnaissance and attacks on shipping. By night his efforts were sporadic. This quiet spell continued throughout January and February, and it was not until the night of March 8th that big-scale air attack flared up.

This attack was directed against Portsmouth, and the enemy's objective was the destruction of certain battleships as they lay in port. Some days before the attack a single scouting 'plane had come over regularly to keep an eye on the battleships. Then, at 7 p.m. on March 8th, the bombers came. Passing Portsmouth to the east, they flew north to Portsdown Hill, where, using the white gash of a quarry as their turning point, they swooped south to the attack. Six separate raids were made before the enemy gave up.

The next night they returned in greater force. Flying in formations of three or four 'planes, they came half an hour later and kept up the attack for four hours. Naval as well as Ack-Ack guns were in action, and their fire was so fierce—the Solent heavy guns alone put up 1,421 rounds—that the bombers gave up diving and had to content themselves with high-level bombing.

They attacked again the next night, for six hours, and received such a pounding from the Solent guns that, although they returned on the following night, the edge had been taken from their determination. Four enemy 'planes were shot down by the guns. The raiders came in from Dieppe at heights varying from 9,000 to 22,000 feet. The night was clear, and the larger bombers could easily be seen silhouetted in the brilliant moonlight. Searchlights had previously been grouped round Portsmouth in pairs in an attempt to put bomb-aimers off their marks by dazzling them. But, although there were four short illuminations, the smoke which was soon rising from many fires hampered this tactic. From 8.47 p.m. fighters were operating over the gun-defended area from 14,000 feet upwards and consequently the guns were not shooting at targets over 12,000 feet. After an hour, however, the guns were again given permission to engage at any height. A feature of the raid was the use of a new type of incendiary bomb which burst 20 or 30 feet above the ground and threw out a shower of blazing magnesium.

Despite the ferocity of the attack—" our concrete command post was rocking like a ship at sea," said one Gun Position Officer—the Gunners had so far gone unscathed. Then, just before the engagement ended, two heavy bombs fell on an A.A. site. One of the bombs landed in the height-finder emplacement and shattered the command post. An officer, a sergeant and nine other ranks were killed. The second bomb fell just outside one of the gun-pits, spraying the crew with splinters and wrecking the hut. Although all the instruments and one of the guns were out of action, and men were trying desperately to save their comrades in the wrecked command post, the Battery continued to engage the enemy with two guns. Captain K. Bermingham and Second-Lieutenant D. Reeds took charge of a gun each—there were not enough men left to man the third—and maintained a steady fire with gun control.

Second-Lieutenant V. Rose was wounded by a bomb splinter which struck the back of his tin hat ; but he continued to rescue men from the wrecked post until he collapsed. He was to lie paralysed in hospital for four months.

Attacks on gun emplacements

When the raiders came again the following night, Major R. N. Guest, Officer Commanding, and Captain Bermingham directed operations not from a command post, which obviously could not be built in time, but from a trestle table set up in the middle of the Gun Park. There, by the light of a hurricane lamp, they sat before a graphic range table measuring out their fuses with a piece of string. A steady flow of hostile 'planes came in from the south and crossed the Solent, most of them continuing northwards to the Midlands. Again there was a clear sky and bright moonlight. H.Es. and incendiaries were dropped over a wide area by 'planes flying between 6,500 and 20,000 feet. At 10 p.m. several anti-personnel bombs fell on one of the gun sites. Most of them fell harmlessly about the camp, but one landed inside a gun emplacement, damaging the gun and killing nine other ranks who were in action at the time. Two officers and three other ranks were wounded. On that night the Solent guns fired a record number of shells—3,653.

During the rest of March there was no big-scale activity over the Solent, although the guns were kept busy firing on ' birds of passage ' bound for the Midlands and the North.

It was on the night of April 17th that the enemy again struck at Portsmouth. Raiders droned over almost without interruption from 9.12 p.m. until 4.25 a.m. Great numbers of bombs were dropped, but the attack misfired badly. Most of the high explosive bombs and incendiaries, with which they sought to wipe out the naval dockyards and the city around them, fell on flat, open fields where they did no harm.

One of the first showers of incendiaries released fell in a half-circle round a gun site. The glare of the blazing incendiaries drew the bombers like moths to a candle flame, and one after another came over to release its load. More than thirty heavy bombs fell on the fields within a quarter of a mile radius of the gun site, but it was not until later in the action that the site was hit. Two fell among the huts, smashing them to matchwood, and a third landed between the command post and the No. 2 gun, which it put out of action, killing some members of the crew. The predictor, in an emplacement next to the Command Post, was also put out of action. A fourth bomb blew in the back of the cabin as the crew sat at the controls. They escaped with a bad shaking.

The Battery continued to engage the enemy 'planes, which were now swooping very low over the position. Some came as low as 600 feet, and one big four-engined bomber was fired on by the guard with their rifles. Two of the remaining three guns went out of action, leaving only the Number 4 gun, christened ' Annie ' by the crew, still firing. Under its Number One, Bombardier Robert Hart, it fired on gun control at parachute flares, hitting three out of six. H.Es. and incendiaries were still being rained on the position, and at last orders were given to evacuate the site.

Before leaving their gun Bombardier Hart and his men made a gesture. They went through the formal drill of going to a standby bearing and marched out of the gun-pit as if they had just finished an hour's silent practice. They then joined the fire-fighting squad.

Six men of the Battery were killed and a number wounded. That the casualties were not far larger was due to the good luck that, though hundreds of incendiaries were dropped, not one fell on the splintered woodwork of the wrecked huts. If they had fallen there they would have lighted a beacon which would have drawn every bomber in the area. During the night the Solent guns claimed two Category I hits (certainly destroyed) and two Category II (probably destroyed). One Junkers 88 crashed with its full bomb-load and blew up. The number of rounds fired by the Solent guns was the highest since the big raid on March 11th—2,771 rounds of 3.7 and 4.5 ammunition.

12. Anti-Aircraft Women

THIS ACCOUNT cannot end without some description of a highly successful experiment which has caught the public fancy more than most other developments of A.A. organisation. This is the introduction of women to form mixed batteries. The first German plane to be shot down by a mixed battery crashed in the Newcastle area on December 8th, 1941. When hit it was a couple of miles away and going out to sea. It was the first proof of a remarkable experiment, the operational significance of which has been obscured by its human interest as well as by a wide range of prejudice.

The first point to bear in mind about women on gun stations is that they are not trained for fun, but because the enemy is at the gates. It is not a whimsical experiment, but a necessary operational plan. The A.A. Command, in common with other services, have a fixed figure which is their man-power ceiling. There are not enough men to go round now, and as the A.A. defences are almost continually increasing, the problem gets more and more difficult.

As early as 1938 General Pile invited Miss Caroline Haslett, the woman engineer, to inspect a battery in the Surrey Hills so that she could give her opinion about women's capacity to do the work. She spent several Sundays there and assured the General that women could do the job. The event has proved her right. Women man everything except the guns themselves in Heavy A.A. units, and man them extremely well. They have the right delicacy of touch, the keenness and the application which is necessary to the somewhat tiresome arts of knob-twiddling which are the lot of the instrument numbers. In principle, also, women will take on all the duties of searchlight detachments. Here again experience has shown that they can be first-class on the job.

The first battery started training in spring, 1940. The A.T.S. members were picked from volunteers, and the men were newly joined recruits, the point being that men who had known no other army life would not find the atmosphere of a mixed battery so hysterically unorthodox. There was considerable anxiety as to how men and women would work together, but there need not have been. They took each other very much for granted ; there was none of the musical-comedy-chorus atmosphere which had been anticipated, partly, no doubt, because such men and women had been working side by side in civilian life for years.

For the outside observer one of the most whimsical features of the whole affair was just this matter of fact atmosphere. The idea of men and women marching, eating, drilling and working together— all this under the auspices of the British army—was not without a certain revolutionary tinge. In a mixed battery, women drive and service the trucks, act as sentries and despatch riders, and, in fact, do everything except fire the guns. Broadly speaking, the men are left with the heavier and dirtier work ; but even this has not led to sex-antagonism. Human nature is not always as ungenerous as cynics claim ; far from resenting the A.T.S., the men in the mixed batteries show a very real pride in the girls' work and are the first to defend them against their critics. One of the most convincing arguments for this experiment is that, the more people have to do with it, the more enthusiastic about it they become.

But we are jumping ahead of the story. In the first mixed battery, as in subsequent batteries, there were more than 200 women and nearly 200 men. Men officers and senior N.C.Os. from established batteries combined with A.T.S. officers to form the nucleus of control. In a mixed battery there are eleven men officers and three A.T.S. officers. The women officers concentrate upon welfare and adminis-tration ; they have nothing to do with the operational side. Opera-tionally the A.T.S. are entirely under the control of male officers, though the latter have no disciplinary powers except that of reporting the girl concerned to her officer. This naturally produces complications, but they have not proved insoluble.

Messing presented certain problems. The new life made these young women very hungry, and the A.T.S. ration was smaller than the men's. Pending an official decision on this point great care was necessary to use the available food to the best advantage. By mutual consent the rations for men and women were pooled and shared equally. The women were well represented on the messing committees. After a while appetites were stabilised, and diet was balanced to provide food popular with both sexes. Special regard was paid to the women's need for fresh fruit, salads and milk foods ; and a balance was found between this and the spotted dog and cheese and pickles beloved of the old soldier—or the new soldier, for that matter.

" *Fit for operational service* "

Naturally this experiment had its troubles ; nothing so funda-mental could be expected to develop without them. But the women surprised their instructors in many ways. In due course they went to finish their initial training at a practice firing camp. The first shooting was more than encouraging. All types of fire control, on all types of heavy equipment were practised, with consistently encouraging results. Here is a practice camp report on a mixed battery, not on the first one where personnel were picked with more than usual care, but an ordinary run-of-the-mill battery. The officer who made it out had an ample basis of comparison. In the previous twenty months he had tested more than a hundred batteries including six mixed batteries ; and this is his routine report on one of them. Other mixed batteries have had better reports ; the particular virtue of this one is that it is typical.

> " Bad weather for the first half of the period slowed up progress, but during the latter half considerable improvement was made. The battery is considered fit for operational service on the equipment they will use. . . .
> " Predictor bearing and angle drill was good, but particularly laying and fuse prediction need practice. Personnel tests should be frequently carried out and the results carefully analysed. Several individual numbers need intensive training, or weeding out, in order that an otherwise good detach-ment will not be spoilt. . . .
> " There is some good material in this battery among the rank and file, both male and female. They have worked hard and made good progress. The turn-out and marching of both men and girls was of a high order. There is an excellent spirit throughout."

In the late summer of 1941 the first of the Mixed Batteries, having completed its initial three-months' training, was sent to an opera-tional site near London and took over its fighting equipment. For the first time women served with men on a war gun-site. Main-tenance of equipment had been a point of some pride during training but with the unit's own equipment a very high standard was set. Soldiers necessarily live hard. Living hard does not mean living uncomfortably, but the soldier relies largely on his own initiative for those comforts he enjoys. In the static life shared by the A.T.S. these considerations do not apply with quite the same force, and although all must keep completely fit, a measure of comfort such as is unobtainable in a mobile theatre can be and is achieved.

Socially the experiment was turning out a great success. The question was how would the women turn out in action ? Gunners firing in action for the first time are inwardly excited but outwardly tense and cool. Would the women be ?

Well, the officer commanding the first mixed battery to bring down a German 'plane said, " As an old soldier, if I were offered the choice of commanding a mixed battery or a male battery, I say without hesitation I would take the mixed battery. The girls cannot be beaten in action, and in my opinion they are definitely better than the men on the instruments they are manning. Beyond a little natural excitement which only shows itself in rather humorous and quaint remarks, they are quite as steady if not steadier than the men. They are amazingly keen at going into action, and although they are not supposed to learn to use the rifle they are as keen as anything to do so.''

This is by no means an isolated reaction. Of course, the novelty has not worn off yet, but the fact emerges that mixed batteries are a very practical proposition.

Women on the searchlights

In April 1941, a searchlight site was manned with A.T.S. under experimental training to see whether they were capable of taking over from men. There were 54 A.T.S., aged from 19 to 35, average age 24. The first three weeks were spent in preparing for the relatively hard, open-air life on a searchlight site. There was much drill and P.T., and five route marches ; also instruction in map reading, anti-gas drill and aircraft recognition. Then came a month's technical training, at the end of which everyone passed the tests : the standard reached was higher than that of most men operating searchlights.

On all except six days, from April 24th to June 19th, there were no sick. The highest number of sick was three, and this for two days only. On 27 days there were a few on light duty, but the number only exceeded four on one occasion. Medical opinion was that personnel could hardly have been fitter.

The women were then moved to a searchlight site to put their training into operation. The first time they exposed their lights on a friendly 'plane there was the usual attack of nerves which happens on these occasions. It is worth noting that the lack of success on the first two night runs had a marked depressing effect. But when, on the tenth night run, operational efficiency was suddenly and rather unexpectedly reached, they were greatly pleased.

The Station was manned for the engagement of enemy aircraft on 18 nights. Enemy aircraft were only engaged twice. There was no result on either night, because the first was early in their training and the second time conditions were not favourable. But the detachment was calm in action, and this calmness was again observed when enemy aircraft were observed machine-gunning a neighbouring site. On four occasions during the experimental period they exposed a homing beacon, and as a result of one of them an aircraft was saved.

Maintenance was better than expected.   Here is an extract from an inspecting officer's report :—

" (a) Generator very clean and serviceable.

" (b) Every item serviceable.

" (c) Lubrication and cleanliness excellent.

" (d) Running test excellent.

" (e) All records up-to-date and well maintained.

" General remarks :

" This generator is one of the cleanest yet inspected.   It is well maintained, easy to start, and obviously the pride of the troop.   It is important to note that this generator is maintained and operated solely by A.T.S. personnel, and it is indeed a credit to them."

The A.T.S. also went in for field engineering, filling and laying sandbags, digging and revetting emplacements. They renovated and reconstructed field works on a derelict searchlight site which was soon to be reoccupied. The work involved shifting several tons of earth, revetting and path-making. By their tenacity of purpose they worked much faster than men and it was particularly observed that they felt no undue fatigue or ill-effects of any sort.

They did guard duty, at first working in pairs by night, but soon getting used to being alone. The tour of duty of sentries was two hours. They were armed with a pick helve, and their main duties were to challenge visitors to the site ; to watch the sky for enemy aircraft and report them ; to report friendly aircraft in distress, and any flares seen ; to log all aircraft flying in the neighbourhood. Spirits were low at first when the results of their work were not very obvious and when it was suggested that they could not stand the winter. Spirits were highest when it was realised that the scheme was a success.

13. Balloons in Battle

AT TEN MINUTES TO NINE on the fine morning of the last day of August 1940, the Germans gave a clear indication of their respect for the British balloon barrage—in their own language. They came across to Dover and shot down every one of the twenty-three balloons flying there in six minutes.

The Battle of Britain had been joined ; and the Dover balloons—which had been deployed during July as a protection against dive bombing—represented the first line of our passive defence. And they still fly in full view of the enemy ; proof of his failure, by this and subsequent attacks, to force us to discontinue the Dover barrage.

The attack began when two waves of about 50 enemy aircraft approached Dover at heights of from 15,000 to 20,000 feet. Six Messerschmitt 109s broke away from these formations and flew at the balloons. This first attack was more successful than any subsequently made, but nevertheless half the force was destroyed ; two aircraft were shot down by anti-aircraft fire and a third by rifle fire from balloon crews.

There were no casualties among the balloon operators, and replacements were immediately put in hand. One crew raised a new balloon within 40 minutes, by 11.30 eleven balloons were flying again over Dover, and by the same afternoon their number was increased to eighteen. At 7.30 in the evening the Germans tried again and shot fifteen more balloons down. But despite these losses, there were sixteen balloons flying over Dover on the following morning.

When these were attacked, three enemy aircraft were shot down at a cost of only two balloons. The crew of a site in the centre of the town lost their balloon but reported as follows : '' The enemy aircraft attacked a balloon which was rising just inflated in the harbour. A 50-round burst of controlled rifle fire staggered the machine, which banked up, clearly disclosing underpart and markings. A second burst of 20 rounds was fired and black smoke was seen coming from the engine, and the machine dived into the sea beyond the break-water.''

Here is another report of the same occurrence. '' On this particular Saturday we were clearing up in the billet when the crackle of machine and cannon guns was heard. Everyone grabbed his rifle and dashed on to the site. The sky was full of A.A. shell bursts while machine guns were going off everywhere. Several balloons were coming down in flames, ours included. The next balloon to us was being hauled down just as fast as the winch could pull it. It was about 800 ft. off the ground when one of the Me. 109s decided that he would try and get it. He swept over our heads and got it all right. But as he turned and banked away to go out to sea again, he seemed to be standing still in the air for a few seconds.

'' The range then was about 700 ft. The N.C.O. in charge yelled ' Fire ! ' Everyone pumped as many rounds as he could into it.

The Me. kept straight on with his dive out to sea, while a thin trail of smoke poured out from behind. When we last saw it, it was going down behind the breakwater out to sea. We didn't have time to stand about wondering if we had got it as we had a new balloon to inflate and fly. This was accomplished in a very short space of time. It was when we had finished this and had the barrage up again that we learnt that we had been given the credit for shooting down a Me.109.''

The attacks proved too costly

The protective balloons still fly over Dover. The attack on the barrage has proved too costly. Subsequent attacks appear to represent individual acts of daring by members of the *Luftwaffe* and are said to be frowned upon by the German authorities. The enemy has been convinced that the game is not worth the candle. The fact, however, that he tried these attacks shows his high opinion of their value and confirmation of this is provided by a special correspondent of the *Giornale d'Italia*, Carlo d'Ongaro, writing from the north coast of France about a raid on Filton carried out by Ober-Leutnant Hollinde.

'' This was one of the most difficult raids carried out by the *Luftwaffe* on England, on account of the exceptional defences at the Filton Works designed to keep off dive bombers. Two rows of balloons were placed round the installations like two concentric circles, and each balloon was very close to the next. They were flying at a height of over 1,200 metres, and their diameter was such that they formed a sort of well into which no pilot in his senses would think of going. Ober-Leutnant Hollinde was aware of the difficulties and for several days he practised aerobatics and worked out the best method of attack. Finally he selected a suitable day with bands of clouds moving across the sky. The buildings at Filton are camouflaged and not easily identified, but the balloon barrage was clearly visible and was useful for locating the target.

'' Hollinde dived down vertically from 3,000 metres and released all the bombs he was carrying : but, although the entry into the balloon well was a practically normal manœuvre for a pilot of his class, entailing only courage and skill, to get out again was another matter. In view of the speed of his aircraft he could not keep on a straight course inside the balloons, and, circling round, he tried to gain height. He was flying so low that he could see the faces of the A.A. gunners, and his gunner fired on the gun crews and on the balloons in turn, but his fire was not sufficient either to silence the guns or to open a way through the balloons. Hollinde then decided

Anti-aircraft women of the A.T.S. operating an identification telescope.

Aircraft recognition is an important feature in the training of A.T.S. girls for mixed batteries.

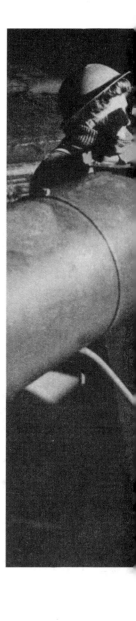

Filming the bursts. A.T.S. check the accuracy of the firing with the Kine-Theodolite.

"Women gunners are not trained for fun." Their work, which demands great skill and endurance, releases a large number of men for front-line service. These girls are manning a range-finder.

" The girls cannot be beaten in action," said the officer commanding a mixed battery. " They are quite as steady, if not steadier, than the men."

to try a dangerous manœuvre and he went into a sideslip and slipped between the balloon cables. Even then he was only inside the second circle, where the balloons were still closer, but he had no time to waste as the daylight was going and he would not have been able to see the cables. Fortunately for him his manœuvre again succeeded and he returned safely to base.''

Finally, William Shirer's *Berlin Diary* records the attitude of German pilots toward the London barrage. '' He (one of the German pilots) relates that they approached London at a height of from 15/16,000 feet, dived to about 10,000 feet and released their bombs at this height—too high for accurate night bombing. They did not dare to go below 7,000 feet, he says, on account of the barrage balloons.''

Baulking the enemy's aim

These two examples of the enemy's opinion of the balloon barrage illustrate its primary object which is to drive the enemy to a height from which accurate bombing is difficult rather than to net him. They indicate too that the barrage is successful either in driving the enemy up or in making him alter his course and disturbing his aim. A report from the Commanding Officer of a naval vessel written in January 1941 stresses the value of balloons in upsetting the aim of attacking bombers.

'' At 10.45 hours on December 27th, while steaming northwards off the North-east Spit Buoy, my ship was attacked by two enemy aircraft. The first bombing attack was turned, apparently by a rather late appreciation of the presence of the balloon barrage, necessitating a sudden swerve on the part of the airmen ; no bombs were dropped. Repeating the attack again from stern, two bombs were dropped about half a cable off my port quarter and it is considered that the balloon prevented a closer attack.''

Apart from attempts at shooting them down the Germans have shown their respect for the balloon barrage in another way. Balloon fenders have been found upon enemy aircraft brought down in this country. This fender is a guard stretching from each wing tip to the nose, and consists of a streamlined shell of light alloy reinforced with a strip of steel along the leading edge, forming a sort of flattened V in front of the aircraft, held in position by five outrigger struts. It is intended that this fender should be strong enough to break the balloon cables by impact or to thrust them aside ; but it weighs about 800 lbs. and reduces the performance of the aircraft very considerably.

Moreover, the fact that enemy bombers are forced to fly high over their targets reduces their chances of avoiding our own fighters and makes them a better target for our anti-aircraft guns. In all these ways therefore the balloon barrage—flying night and day through the most severe aerial bombardments—has made a positive contribution to the safety of our cities, ports, dockyards and factories, and the fact that our industrial effort has remained so largely unimpaired is in no small measure due to the dogged maintenance of this form of passive defence.

14. Stockade to Barrage

Balloon Defence Grows

THE CONCEPTION of balloons as a weapon of air defence originated before the last war. The general idea, then, was to build a stockade of nets in the skies and thus enmesh hostile aircraft on their way to a defended area. The Germans also tried a form of balloon or kite barrage as early as the winter of 1914/15. By March 1917 they were forming balloon barrage detachments to protect important industrial establishments. Our aircraft did not often encounter the enemy barrage, but in January 1918 a British F.E.2b of No. 100 Squadron (pilot, Second-Lieutenant L. G. Taylor ; observer, Second-Lieutenant F. E. Le Fevre) was caught in such a net on the way back from Trèves. The pilot and observer were taken prisoner, but the pilot made a full report of his experiences after the war, emphasising the fearful mess which the balloon cable had made of his machine.

One of the earliest Allied barrages was in Venice, where there were seven stations each with ten balloons. These were inflated during each moonlight period and flown from rafts at about 10,000 feet, at distances of just over 200 feet apart, around the city. In June 1917 a Royal Flying Corps officer was sent to Italy to report on the scheme. And on September 5th of that year Major-General E. B. Ashmore, who commanded the London Air Defence Area, put forward his scheme for a London balloon barrage. He suggested an apron consisting of a row of balloons connected by a cross cable carrying weighted wire streamers. His scheme was approved by the Government, and he arranged at once to instal two balloon aprons on the easterly borders of London each consisting of five Caquot balloons disposed in a straight line 2,000 yards in length, with the balloons anchored to the ground at three points and linked together by cable from which wire streamers 1,000 feet long were suspended.

In October the Commander-in-Chief, Home Forces, agreed to the establishment of a Home Wing of five balloon squadrons with a total establishment of 3,587 personnel, at the same time giving his approval for " the installation of a cordon of 20 balloon aprons, approximately on the line, Tottenham—Ilford—Barking—Woolwich and Lewisham, subject to such modifications as experience may suggest." By April 1918 seven of the aprons were in operation and an eighth was nearly ready.

The balloon aprons acted as a kind of stockade against enemy aircraft. Their position was carefully checked by our own fighter patrols and the closest co-operation with anti-aircraft guns and searchlights existed. The stockade of balloons was, however, heavy and inflexible. It was difficult to operate, and its weight was a potential menace to the population it was designed to protect. Its value as a reassurance to the civilian population was, however, apparent. In the words of Major-General Ashmore reporting on May 27th, 1918. " In my opinion, the balloon aprons are an essential part of the defence ; to do away with them would have the worst possible effect. Our aircraft patrols would have to cover all heights instead of a comparatively narrow zone as at present. London would certainly be bombed from low heights at which considerable accuracy is attainable."

The success of the balloon aprons as a scarecrow is borne out by the records of the enemy. In March 1918 a report was made to General von Hoeppner to the effect that " the aprons had increased enormously, and that they added greatly to the difficulties of the attack. If they were increased and improved much more they would make a raid on London almost impossible." In the same month a German prisoner stated that the aprons were " sufficient to keep all machines at their maximum height." All reports from German sources in fact stressed the nervousness felt by their airmen toward the balloon aprons.

The plan behind the barrage

When the barrage was hauled down in 1918, work on defensive balloons lapsed, though an establishment was always maintained for experimental purposes. The necessity of having to organise and maintain a barrage in any future war was represented by the Air Defence of Great Britain Command at various times between 1928 and 1935. Finally, the Air Staff decided in 1936 to establish a barrage in London, the question of provincial barrages being left

open until some experience had been gained of the working of the
barrage in the Metropolis.

A ring of balloons flying at a radius of about seven and a half miles
from Charing Cross was first envisaged as a layout for the London
barrage. The balloons were to be spaced ten to a mile, giving
a total of 450 balloons at approximately 200 yard intervals. The
stockade idea had been abandoned. The new barrage was con-
ceived as flexible, each balloon being independent and mobile.

To this end a preliminary survey of the 45-mile circle round
London was undertaken. But almost before it had started the idea
of " perimeter siting " was abandoned in favour of " field siting."
Balloons dotted all over a protected area would, obviously, force
an attacking aircraft to fly above them all the time. If, however,
the original idea had been carried out the aircraft need only have
flown over the protecting screen when it would have been able to
come in as low as it liked to make its attack.

At this stage the question of operational height had to be considered. A balloon has to lift not only its own weight but also the
weight of its cable. The higher a balloon is to fly, therefore, the
greater must be its volume to give it lifting capacity. No doubt the
ideal would be to fly balloons at such a height that enemy aircraft
could never fly over them, but this would mean a balloon so large
that it would be extremely difficult to handle on the ground, particularly in a built-up area. It was therefore decided to operate balloons
at medium heights, preventing accurate aiming and dive-bombing
and at the same time leaving the upper air free for fighter
interception.

It would have been uneconomical in peace-time to maintain a
permanent strength of operators for the full London barrage.
Moreover, the presence of so many balloons in and around London
would have been too great a menace to peace-time air traffic. An
auxiliary organisation on the same lines as that of the Territorial
army was, therefore, introduced.

The Balloon Squadrons were to be manned principally by
auxiliaries able to do part-time or week-end training in association
with a small nucleus of regular personnel and concentrated in four
main depots in the metropolitan area to be defended. These centres
were the first meeting grounds of the many who volunteered their
services and who still maintain protective barrages throughout the
country at the present day. They were used both as storage depots
and for training the squadrons which would be deployed to their
own war sites in the event of war. To-day the centres are used as
maintenance and supply depots for squadrons in the field.

The majority of the balloons for use in war were stored and packed in these centres, a small number being kept inflated for training and test purposes. The selection of suitable positions for the centres in the crowded environs of London presented great difficulty in itself. An area of up to 80 acres was required, situated within reasonable distance of the war sites, accessible for auxiliaries travelling from their homes in spare time, and not too close to existing airfields to interfere with flying.

Early in 1938 work was started, and the recruiting of the first balloon squadrons commenced. A balloon training school was opened, and a nucleus of regular personnel was given an intensive course of training before being posted to the various centres. A balloon group headquarters under Fighter Command was also formed to control and administer the barrage as a whole and Air Commodore J. G. Hearson took up his appointment as the first Air Officer Commanding.

At the time of the international crisis in September 1938 the organisation was sufficiently developed to permit a partial mobilisation of the barrage and some squadrons were deployed fully equipped to their war sites. They remained on a war footing for about ten days, but were eventually withdrawn after a useful exercise had been carried out.

The performance of the London barrage units had, indeed, been so satisfactory that it was decided to proceed with the establishment of barrages in many of the important provincial cities. The first to be chosen were Portsmouth, Southampton, Plymouth, Bristol, Cardiff, Swansea, Liverpool, Manchester, Glasgow, Newcastle, Sheffield, Hull, Birmingham and Coventry. And with this expansion came the decision to establish a separate Balloon Command.

Early in 1939 the provincial groups were established on a skeleton basis, and sufficient progress had been made by September to enable the barrage for the whole country to be mobilised.

15. When the Balloon Goes Up

AT THE OUTBREAK of war a small group assembled on the roof of the Air Ministry in Whitehall to watch the first wartime barrage make its appearance. Punctually to the minute it rose into the clear autumn skies. At once logical and preposterous, comforting and extraordinary, these first balloons were made welcome as a new aspect of city life. Throughout the length and breadth of the country their crews and the public hastened to christen them. Within three days of the beginning of war, a balloon flying above an archbishop's palace was locally known as the ' Archblimp.' More often a feminine name was regarded for some reason as appropriate. The balloon and its successors at the Dover site whose crew shot down the Messerschmitt with their rifles are called ' Matilda.' The advent of W.A.A.F. balloon crews recently started a more romantic fashion in names. The first W.A.A.F. crew to operate in London christened their charge ' Romeo.'

The balloon barrage is nowadays so familiar that we tend to take it for granted. In fact its maintenance calls for the exercise of much individual skill and for much organisation behind the scenes.

The usual type of barrage balloon is a streamlined bag of rubber-proofed cotton fabric, specially treated, with a gas capacity of 19,150 cubic feet, a length overall of about 63 feet, and a height of just over 31 feet. It weighs approximately 550 lbs. and it is flown on a flexible steel cable. On the outbreak of war it took at least 40 minutes for any single balloon to rise into the air ; it now takes less than 20 minutes. Such is the progress achieved in a new and by no means easy technique.

Balloons rise because they are filled with hydrogen which is many times lighter than air. Now if 1 cubic foot of hydrogen gas rises, the ever diminishing atmospheric pressure will cause it to expand. In fact if it reached a height of 19,000 feet it would expand to 2 cubic feet. Increases in temperature also cause expansion. Allowance must therefore be made for gas expansion at operational flying levels.

The French made their balloons with elastic sides, but this did not work well in practice. The envelopes of British balloons have ' false bottoms ' filled with air which is expelled as soon as the gas chamber expands. This ' false bottom ' is known as the ballonet, and the flexible wall which separates it from the gas chamber is the diaphragm. When a balloon is inflated at ground level, the upper compartment is not filled to capacity with gas and the ballonet is filled with air through its wind scoop. The balloon goes up, the atmospheric pressure decreases, and the expanding gas presses the air out of the ballonet. As the balloon descends, the ballonet scoops back air when the gas contracts. So the shape of the balloon remains constant and the three air-inflated stabilizers, like two huge fins and a rudder, enable the balloon to ride head-to-wind always on an even keel.

These are the rudiments of a barrage balloon. But there is a highly specialised and constantly improving technique in flight—manipulation, close-hauling, bedding down, and always, day and night, getting the best of the weather.

The answer was a millstone

At the outbreak of war all balloons were flown directly from the leading-off gear at the back of their winches, all of which were motorised. To moor the balloon on the ground it was necessary to peg out a wire bed and manually to haul the balloon down, after it had been brought to within a few yards of the ground, by means of handling guys and a rope tackle.

With every change of wind the balloon had to be let up from its bed into its flying position while the bed was re-laid, because it is essential to keep a balloon head to wind. This was often impossible in turbulent weather, particularly at night and the only alternative was to leave the balloon broadside to the wind and pray for the dawn. In November 1939, this resulted in a 50 per cent. casualty rate throughout the entire barrage.

Such a problem had never arisen before. Observation balloon operators in the past could choose their sites and their weather. The new barrage principle of field siting allowed no such power of selection. Clearly an all-directional bed was necessary upon which a balloon could be turned in all weathers without releasing its moorings or moving the winch.

The answer was a homely millstone purchased for a few pence from a Borough Council yard. It was pushed through Hampstead by a balloon crew and rolled on to the sacrosanct turf of Hampstead Cricket Club. Almost between the creases a pit was dug, into which the millstone was rolled with a chain reeved through it. The hole was filled up and the turf replaced, leaving only a few links of the chain above ground to which an ordinary cable pulley was attached. From this pulley the balloon was actually flown, and the winch was withdrawn to an onlooker's position at the side of the ground. The all-directional bed where the balloon could be safely moored in all weathers and kept head to wind was provided by a rope or wire cradle and wire mooring circle now generally used throughout Great Britain.

The rope cradle consists of 12 rope legs attached to the central anchorage. The ends of these legs are loaded with sandbags, to which the balloon is attached by means of tensioning slips. When the balloon is to be turned, the rope cradle and bags are dragged round by hand, and the handling guys and picketing lines by which the balloon is moored are stepped round one at a time in the direction which the balloon is to follow.   In this manner the balloon can be turned without running the many risks of releasing it from its bed. The familiar array of sandbags on balloon sites was replaced later by concrete ballast blocks which are easier to handle, are neater and last a lot longer.

A more recent improvement is the tail-guy mooring which enables the balloon to be moored with its stabilizers filled with air ready to be raised at a moment's notice. This achieves a state of readiness throughout the barrage which is of the greatest operational importance. It enables the balloon, without resort to the use of handling guys, to be held at two points only—by the flying rigging at the point of attachment and at the stern of the balloon itself by the tail guy. The tail guy is attached to a wire circle about 180 feet in diameter, and it is simply shifted along the perimeter wire when it is desired to turn the balloon head to wind.

Lightning gets them down

In tolerable weather balloons can be left flying on the tail-guy mooring, and several minutes can be saved in raising each balloon into the air : but in really turbulent weather they are better bedded down.

Amid the vagaries of the British climate the flying of thousands of balloons presents an hourly struggle with the weather. One of the greatest potential dangers is lightning. At four o'clock on an afternoon in February 1939, only two flashes of lightning were recorded in the whole of Great Britain. But one destroyed a balloon at Stanmore, the other a balloon at Chigwell. Captive balloons, attached as they are to the end of a metal cable which forms in itself an efficient lightning conductor, were found, in fact, to be very vulnerable to lightning if flown during thunderstorms ; and, as hydrogen is a highly inflammable gas, they don't last long if they are struck.

During the autumn of 1939 as many as 80 balloons were burned in the air in one afternoon in London alone. Arrangements were therefore made for weather forecasts of thundery conditions to be supplied throughout Balloon Command, and as many balloons as possible are now bedded down when there is danger of lightning. In view of the very localised nature of thunderstorms this policy would, if followed rigidly, result in unnecessary curtailment of flying. Moreover the tactical situation at times may demand that balloons should be flown in thunderstorms. It was, therefore, essential for lightning protection to be provided, and widespread investigations were undertaken, in the course of which balloon crews themselves gave valuable help in handling the scientific instruments used.

As a result a practical form of lightning protection has been devised which, whilst not giving complete immunity, does minimise the risk. The results of the experiments also led to the construction of an instrument which uses any electrical currents flowing in the balloon cable to give warning of the approach of highly dangerous conditions. When in fact a balloon is struck by lightning, the electricity passes to earth through the winch or anchorage from which the balloon is flown. Members of a crew near the foot of the cable therefore have to take precautions, and these have been designed and thoroughly tested on the largest electrical discharges which can be artificially produced. Amongst the precautions which are now routine practice on all sites, is that of always jumping on to or off a winch in order to avoid conducting a discharge. This and other precautions minimise a very real danger to balloon crews.

16. The Crews that Man Them

A BALLOON crew originally consisted of two corporals and ten men ; but progress in balloon manipulation has made it possible to reduce the crew to two corporals and eight men. These numbers allow for leave, sickness and absence on courses and in practice a corporal and five airmen can manage a balloon satisfactorily. The necessity for maintaining a constant guard by day and night takes up much of their time, however, and makes it impossible to reduce the size of the crew.

In spite of the fact that the speed of operation has been enormously increased, the physical labour entailed in manipulation has decreased in many ways. In early days the public was familiar with the sight of a balloon crew hauling the balloon down from ten yards or so off the ground to its bed by means of a rope tackle. This operation is now carried out by means of a windlass on the side of the winch, and in many other ways manual work has been eliminated.

Nevertheless a balloon crew has an exceedingly full day, as is illustrated by the words of a balloon operator in the centre of London :

" ' Come on—ten to two ! ' With these few choice words I find myself rudely awakened from my warm blanket bed to go on Guard for two hours. Having completed this duty and being relieved, I crawl back to bed and attempt to get a three hours' sleep. At 07.00 hours the Mess Orderly for the day awakens me along with the remainder of the Crew, to commence our many varied duties of the day. After breakfast, having done my share of cleaning the billet, personal equipment and rifle, I proceed to Flight Headquarters to collect three thousand bricks to bring back and unload on my site, where the remainder of the Crew are digging up the turf to a depth of six inches and laying a brick bed.

"I make my way back to the site in time for tea (16.30 hours). After a much-needed wash, I proceed to look at the Guard List (the ever-present duty) finding myself 'fixed' for two hours from 22.00 hrs. to 23.59 hrs. This regular happening is unavoidable. After cleaning myself up I make my bed and take the opportunity of an hour or two of leisure before my Guard. At 22.30 hours I report to the Visiting Duty Officer, and at 23.45 hrs., just as I am preparing to be relieved after a last walk round the site, an Operational broadcast is received giving an order to bed down the balloon, due to bad weather. I turn the Crew out and finally, after completing this operation, I retire to my much-needed bed."

The daily routine duties

They don't have to deal with three thousand bricks every day but, apart from this, they have obviously plenty to do. Much time is spent on maintenance. The daily routine duties carried out on a site include the following:

Operational orders to fly, alter height, close-haul or bed the balloon. Switch on or off Rip Link.

Daily Inspections.

Keeping Balloon head to wind on the bed, Tail Guy Mooring or Interim Close-haul.

Maintenance of Balloon : Repairs and Topping-up.

    ,,   ,,   Winch : Cleaning and Brake tests. Winch Tool Maintenance and Check.

    ,,   ,,   Bed : Blocks, Tackle, Bedwires, Pyramid, Cradle, Sandbags, Slips, Ragbolts, " U " bolts, Ringbolts, Screw pickets, 90-foot Circle and Strops, Tail Guy Snatchblock, Central Anchorage Snatchblock.

    ,, . ,,   Flying Cable : Oil and inspect throughout.

Inspection and Maintenance of Armaments.

Gas Drill.

Defence and Weapon Training.

Lay-out of Kits and Bedding.

Maintenance and Cleaning of Personal Kit.

Messing Fatigues and Site Cooking.

Inspection and Maintenance of Gas Cylinders, Trailer, Topping-up and Inflation Equipment.

Balloon crews were accommodated in the early days in tents and fed on rations supplied in hay boxes from central kitchens. Accommodation is now usually in hutments : to an increasing extent food is cooked on the spot.

The following account from one of the auxiliaries who took part in the first deployment of the provincial barrages recalls the atmosphere of those first days of war.

" War declared—fly all balloons, and the sixteen balloons of two flights of the first squadron of Manchester rose as one, simultaneously with London. The billets here, there and everywhere, improvised, cajoled, demanded. High-hat houses, mean houses, factory floors —no blankets, no huts, no tents, nothing. Millions of children and thousands of irate ladies indicating that they could not feed and house 12 lusty men for ever for nothing. But the balloons flew— came down somehow, and went up somehow. Improvise, manage, do without, get hot, get cold, get hungry, stay hungry, Office work started, telephones used at the local grocer's, Flight H.Q. in the local pub, provided with piles of pennies for calls. But the balloons flew, and more balloons. The auxiliaries who stuck all this with us were mostly not young. The butcher, baker, banker—all did their damnedest."

The W.A.A.F. takes over

In the middle of January 1941, the Air Officer Commanding, Balloon Command, was asked to consider a suggestion that the flying of balloons could be completely carried out by the W.A.A.F. At first this suggestion was received with some dismay. The fact that the manning of balloons for 24 hours a day, frequently in the most appalling weather conditions, required physical strength not generally possessed by women, was considered in itself sufficient reason for rejecting it.

Nevertheless, the Air Officer Commanding examined the problem with the utmost care. Every aspect of the suggestion was explored, from the physical suitability of women as balloon operators to the

accommodation that they would require ; from the amount of food
to be issued to them to the type of clothes they would have to wear ;
from the strength of W.A.A.F. crews to the question of whether or
not they should use lethal weapons.   After a great deal of thought
an experiment was finally made to see just what the airwomen of
the W.A.A.F. could, or could not, do when they got on to a balloon
site.

Thus one cold, wet morning in April 1941, 20 W.A.A.F. Balloon
Fabric workers, all volunteers, dressed in oilskins and sou'westers,
marched on to a training site at a balloon centre just outside London.
There, under the guidance of eight R.A.F. balloon operators, and
watched by a group of senior R.A.F. technical and medical officers,
they carried out a number of simple balloon operations for the first
time.   The experiment, like the rain, lasted all day.   But at the end
of it the W.A.A.F. emerged successfully.

A month later the first batch of W.A.A.F.—again all volunteers
and mostly balloon-fabric workers—were posted to the largest
balloon training centre in the country for ten weeks intensive
training.   At the end of the course the W.A.A.F. Balloon Operators
were once more put through their paces for the benefit of senior
R.A.F. Officers.

The scene on this occasion was very different from that wet
morning in April.   Sun had taken the place of rain.   The oilskins
and sou'westers had disappeared, and in their place the airwomen
wore smart air-force-blue working suits.   The pale faces of yesterday
were now tanned by the July sun.   And most important of all, the
enthusiastic but inexperienced W.A.A.F. of April were now carrying out the complicated balloon operations with all the ease and
efficiency of the R.A.F.

A few days later the Air Officer Commanding was able to report
to the Secretary of State for Air : '' Training has proceeded to the
extent that it has now been found possible to draft women to war
sites in the Balloon Barrage, which sites they will in a few days' time
be in course of taking over from the airmen.''   Every week since
then the W.A.A.F. have taken over more and more balloon sites.
They will continue to do so until a very large proportion of the
Balloon Barrages in the British Isles will be manned by airwomen,
the airmen being remustered to, or trained for, more arduous jobs.

The substitution of W.A.A.F. for airmen on balloon sites does
not imply that the airmen, who have operated in all weathers and
under aerial bombardment, have in any sense been doing a '' woman's
job.''   In the first place, it requires a crew of 16 airwomen to replace
10 airmen.   Secondly, it must be borne in mind that R.A.F. crews

are incorporated in military defence schemes, whereas W.A.A.F. are not. Thus, in a number of areas it is not practicable for W.A.A.F. to take over sites. Lastly, it is only the great progress in and simplification of balloon manipulation, for which the original officers and airmen of Balloon Command are responsible, that has made the substitution at all possible. ⁻Skill and intelligence will still be required, but the constant physical strain which was present in the past has been very much reduced.

The Balloon Operators of the W.A.A.F. will still have to endure the weather as well as attack from the air, but they have already shown that they can take it. Theirs is undoubtedly one of the hardest jobs undertaken by women in this war, but they have tackled it and succeeded at it.

17. "A Jerry went smack into my cable"

O N T H E first day of war the London Balloon Barrage flew practically complete, but the Provinces were still short of balloons. At the beginning of September 1939, barrages were deployed and flying at the following, amongst other places :

LONDON	MANCHESTER	PLYMOUTH
BIRMINGHAM	BRISTOL	CARDIFF
COVENTRY	HULL	NEWCASTLE
DERBY	SOUTHAMPTON	SHEFFIELD
LIVERPOOL	PORTSMOUTH	GLASGOW

During the last three months of 1939 the following barrages were deployed for the first time :

FORTH   CREWE   THAMES and HARWICH

In February 1940, the Scapa Barrage was formed, and during May and June several factory barrages were added. In July the South Wales barrages were strengthened. In addition to balloons sited on land, many balloons were flown from vessels moored in harbours and estuaries, to protect vulnerable points and areas round the coast.

In spite of difficulties, and thanks to an inherent talent for improvisation, the balloons flew ; and the size of the British barrage has grown from hundreds to thousands. To-day this barrage is a vital link in the air defence of the country, a main girder in the " Roof over Britain."

The Air Officer Commanding-in-Chief, Fighter Command, is responsible in the first place for the operational control of the balloon barrage. The Chain of Command is derived from him as follows :

THE AIR OFFICER COMMANDING-IN-CHIEF, FIGHTER COMMAND
THE AIR OFFICER COMMANDING, BALLOON COMMAND
BALLOON GROUPS
BARRAGE CONTROL
SQUADRONS
FLIGHTS
SITES

Fighter Groups throughout the United Kingdom may also initiate operations through the Balloon Groups.

In addition to general operational control and to the exigencies of the weather, barrages are naturally subject to some local control. Those operating in the neighbourhood of an aircraft base, for instance, are subject to the local flying control authorities ; those guarding aircraft factories often provide controllable lanes through which aircraft may be admitted to the factory landing ground.

Impact of hostile aircraft

Though their main function is to " position the pheasant," our balloons have been directly responsible for bringing down enemy aircraft. The first such aircraft to be claimed by a British balloon in this war was one brought down by the barrage flown at Le Havre in June 1940.

During January 1942, a new type of German bomber was destroyed in a barrage in the North-east of England. The balloon crew heard the aircraft approaching their site very fast and low ; then they heard their balloon cable struck, but it was too dark to see the aircraft. The bomber crashed between one and two miles farther on, and the balloon cable was recovered intact. A portion of the starboard wing of the enemy plane, cleanly cut by the impact, was subsequently recovered from a neighbouring site. The airman in charge of the site said, a day or two later :

" I've been putting balloons up and down, down and up, up and down, since October, 1939, but it wasn't till this week that a real live Jerry went smack into my cable. It was just about getting dark when we got orders to fly our balloons. In a few minutes she was off the bed and aloft. We were rather pleased with ourselves, the boys and me, for we had put it up in extra quick time. I remember saying to one of the blokes, ' If we don't get Annie up soon we'll probably be too late.' I was only joking really, because we had put our Annie up scores of times without even hearing an enemy 'plane.

" Well, when she was up, we trooped off back to our hut leaving the duty picquet on guard. We'd just started to listen to the radio when we heard the 'plane coming low—very low it was, much too low for my liking—so we decided to get outside and get a bit of cover. That's the worst of our job : you can't hit back at 'em. You've just got to sit and take it. We'd no sooner got outside than the noise of the 'plane changed to a whine. It seemed just as if it was diving right down on top of us.

" ' Jeanny Macke ! ' says one of our airmen—an Irishman who says things like that when he's roused. ' Jeanny Macke ! ' he says. ' He's going to machine gun us.'

" ' He isn't,' says I. ' He's going to hit the cable.'

" And he did. He went smack into it. There was a crash, and the old winch jumped as she took the strain. The cable sawed through the wing just like a grocer's wire goes through cheese. That fixed him. Off came the best part of a wing and we knew we'd got him. After a few seconds, about a thousand yards away from us, we saw a big red glow. We couldn't go and have a dekko for it's against orders to leave the site when you are on duty, but we heard from our Flight Commander that the 'plane had crashed and was burning like a Brock's Benefit. Flames lit the whole sky and Very lights were popping off every minute.

" We celebrated our first Jerry with a nice cup of tea. Then we realised we'd got to put up another balloon in place of Annie, because, of course, Annie didn't live here any more. She'd done her job pretty well, we thought, and we were sorry to see her go, but, mind you, we weren't complaining. We had had our bit of excitement and our two years of waiting had been well rewarded. It took us until the early hours of the following morning to put our new balloon up, and then we went to bed feeling rather pleased with ourselves.''

In the small hours of the morning of September 13th, 1940, a Heinkel impacted the cable of a balloon flying in Newport, South Wales. The aircraft swung round and the cable was pulled out and off the storage drum. The aircraft flew on towards another site with the cable clinging to it. This fouled the cable on the second site and the aircraft crashed and burst into flames.

It is comparatively rare, however, for the crews to have the great satisfaction of catching the enemy in their cables. Destroying him is for the fighters and the guns. But balloon crews know that they can help by keeping the balloons aloft whatever the weather and whatever the aerial bombardment in progress, and this they have done—never better, perhaps, than on the night of November 14th, 1940 at Coventry. This is the report afterwards written by the Squadron Commander on the spot.

Coventry was the target

" The brilliant, almost full moon shone down on a city where life and business went on just the same despite frequent visits from Göring's *Luftwaffe*. In the Barrage Control Office at Squadron Headquarters, officers and men watched the plotting table with not a little anxiety, for a constant stream of enemy 'planes were plotted as heading for Coventry. The warning was received at 19.11 hours. In spite of the weather risk, the Barrage Commander ordered that the balloons should be flown at staggered operational height.

" The enemy attack commenced at 19.30 and continued with terrific intensity until about 06.30 hours next morning. The first raiders dropped showers of incendiary bombs which started fires in the city. These were clearly visible from 916 S.H.Q. Guided by this ' beacon,' waves of enemy aircraft flew over the city, dropping large quantities of high explosives. It soon became obvious that this was an attack greater in intensity than any previously experienced. The first balloon inflated (new site) was reported at 19.27 hours. This was quickly followed up by similar reports as each site raised its balloon.

" At 20.30 hours telephonic communication broke down completely and Squadron Headquarters were out of touch with Flights and Sites. Despatch riders were rapidly brought into service, and, under conditions of greatest difficulty and danger, they worked for the remainder of the night. In some places it was only possible to get through on foot. Then came another catastrophe. All lighting failed. Emergency lighting was brought into use at once."

Throughout the night, Flight Headquarters and Sites were experiencing trouble. The following are extracts from Flight Commanders' reports :

" We have a small shelter capable of accommodating six people, we had six civilians and four children in it. A near miss blew in the windows of Flight Headquarters and brought down the roof. We had to evacuate."

A Pilot Officer from " B " Flight Headquarters says : " I was making a round of sites in my car ; as I left Site 17 a bomb dropped about 100 yards ahead bringing down two houses. I stopped the car.

Putting the balloons to bed in giant hangars is part of the intensive training undertaken by balloon operators.

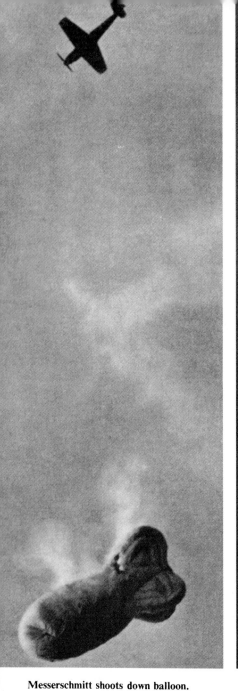

Messerschmitt shoots down balloon.

A balloon is struck by lightning.

The convoy flies its protecting barrage. These balloons, manned by R.A.F. crews, offer a serious obstacle to the dive-bomber. They are smaller and easier to handle than those of our land defences. *Below*—A depot barge of the Kite Balloon Section. Sea-going balloons were at one time painted in a diced pattern for camouflage purposes.

The W.A.A.F. takes over. The handling of barrage balloons requires skill, teamwork and considerable physical strength.

Then two women came running to the car, asking me to help them. I took the ladies to ' B ' Flight Headquarters, gave them a stimulant and put them in the shelter. Then I took the ambulance and picked up a number of people who had been hurt.'' The report goes on to say : '' The Flight Commander went out to where a delayed-action bomb had fallen 70 yards from Headquarters. He would not allow anyone to go near it and took care of the boarding-up himself.'' Special mention is also made of two airmen, of whom it is said : '' They would not take shelter and their tireless work in visiting the Sick Quarters and organising generally was invaluable.''

An Officer at '' B '' Flight makes the following observations : '' All the windows of our Headquarters were blown in and several D/A bombs fell within a few yards. Huts on sites 18 and 40 were destroyed. The crew of site 18 evacuated to their dug-out, but a D/A fell adjacent to the wall of the dug-out and they had to leave that, too. When a delayed-action bomb fell about 10 yards from the bed of Site 8, the men were in their Anderson shelter, but on hearing the balloon cable was falling, they turned out, hauled down the balloon and bedded it. Then they returned to their shelter. From '' D '' Flight comes the news that the '' blitz '' started whilst a new balloon was being inflated. The crew of Site 59 had to leave the inflation and deal with incendiaries.''

A message came to Flight Headquarters from the First Aid Post 40 yards away, that they wanted help to change the punctured wheels of ambulances. All the R.A.F. drivers and the Flight Commander gave a hand. Afterwards seven men volunteered to help with First Aid. Later, personnel from '' D '' Flight set off for Coventry in buses and ambulances, helped to evacuate people and to dig other luckless victims out of shelters.

When the ' Raiders Passed ' signal was sounded the Balloon Barrage set about replacing its many casualties. Many problems had to be faced. The complete breakdown of telephonic communication and the blocking of the roads were not easily overcome. In spite of the many casualties and obvious difficulties encountered, the Balloon Barrage was up to strength and flying by 12.00 hours on November 16th, 1940.

The part played by the Officers, N.C.Os. and men of Coventry's Balloon Barrage was quiet and unspectacular, but it was definitely a contribution—and a very real contribution—to the part played by the people of Coventry in the most terrible attack Britain had ever experienced.

18. Balloons at Sea

TO COMPLETE the circle of protection of harbours and estuaries, balloons are sometimes flown from surface craft moored on the water. Water-borne barrages not only afford protection to vulnerable areas and to shipping, but they also have the greatest value as a deterrent to mine-laying by the enemy.

On Christmas Day the Commanding Officer of a water-borne squadron set out with his Adjutant in a launch to shake the hand of every balloon operator under his charge. Without stopping for more than the usual Christmas greeting anywhere, this trip took him four and a half hours. This illustrates the practical difficulties of maintaining a whole barrage afloat. Nevertheless some of the most useful work carried out by Balloon Command is upon the water.

Life in the water-borne barrage varies with the geographic situation. In a typical estuary barrage, the balloons are flown from barges and drifters. Each of these vessels is mobile and keeps steam up day and night. There is a civilian crew for manœuvring the vessel, and a crew of three or four airmen, with a Corporal in charge, to manipulate the balloon. The winch is generally contained in the hold of the vessel, and as, of course, there is no means of bedding down, the balloons must always remain either flying or else close-hauled. A period of ten days to a fortnight at sea is usual. During this period the crews may be in sight of land, but their only connection is the daily visit of the ration boat and the radio watch they keep. More frequently than those of any other balloon site these men have had opportunities of combat with the enemy. Several hostile aircraft have been brought down by their gunfire.

Very few individual members of these balloon crews had been at sea before joining the barrage, and it usually takes some days for them to find their sea-legs and accustom themselves to the considerable motion set up in a craft moored in tidal estuaries. In spite of this, they take to the life enthusiastically and have made their quarters habitable and shipshape. Except for transfer to air-crew duties, very rarely do any of them seek a shore job.

The manufacture of models, carpentry and metal-work seem to occupy such spare time as they have, though they have all become successful and enthusiastic fishermen.

During the Battle of Britain in August, 1940 it was essential that the English Channel should remain open to our Convoys. On

August 4th a Convoy left a West of England port for the Thames Estuary protected for the first time by balloons of Balloon Command. The Royal Navy also maintains balloons upon H.M. ships and Merchant ships at sea, but the story of their fine work must be told elsewhere than in a description of Britain's defensive roof.

During that first trip and nearly every subsequent trip the balloons were attacked by Messerschmitt fighters. Through rain, snow, ice and fog, in gales, in winds which threatened almost to tear the winches from the decks, the Royal Air Force crews of Balloon Barrage vessels make their trips round the coast. They have, of course, seen more action than any other balloon crews and they have already won many awards for gallantry and good service.

Enemy fighters are not the only resistance encountered. Shells from German batteries are often observed. On one occasion one of these severed a balloon cable.

The following extracts from the log of an R.A.F. officer on a balloon barrage vessel indicate the variety of the hazards run in affording this protection :

" **0950 hours.** Mine sighted on port bow necessitating sudden change of course. This was followed by sighting other mines on the starboard bow until eventually we zig-zagged through 23 of them. Obviously they had broken loose during the storm.

" **1105 hours.** An Me.109 made two machine-gun attacks on ' ——.' Shooting bad and no hits. ' —— ' attacked by four dive-bombers. Bombs could be seen hitting the sea beside the ship.

" **1856 hours.** Vivid flashes from French coast.

" **2143 hours.** Enormous flash from French coast followed some 80 seconds later by the sound of heavy explosion.

" **2224 hours.** A.A. fire from French coast. Throughout the night there was a series of flashes and occasional A.A. fire from both coasts.

" **Thursday. 0220 hours.** This has been written subsequently, as things moved too fast to record them at the time. I came below to call my relief, and as I came on deck again I was told that a motor boat had been heard on our port bow and had disappeared. About five minutes later there was an explosion astern followed immediately by another.

" Immediately the place seemed to become like a Brock's firework display. Everybody who had anything seemed to let it off. Tracers showing up scarlet in the night were returned by bullets which appeared green in colour. We kept dead quiet. The trouble was—

or appeared to be—about a quarter of a mile astern, and we were in a position that we could do nothing effective if we did open fire.

" What actually happened we shall not know till we reach port, but the Motor Torpedo Boat Brigade were putting up flares all over the place. Presently we heard a ' phew '—almost next door it seemed—but whatever it was, it did not find its mark. After what seemed hours, but was only a few minutes, it seemed that the firework party was falling astern.

" Personally, I heaved a sigh of relief. By the gun flashes and rattle of machine guns I knew our escort was doing its stuff. But suddenly right on our starboard beam two high flares shot up and came sailing down lighting ' —— ' and ourselves as clear as day. There followed what we all expected—a sickening thud. We thought the ' —— ' had got it. Then there was another lull, followed by the usual cries of ' There she is ' as machine guns opened up again and flares showed us up.

" Suffice it to say that I think all of us were glad when dawn broke and we could see ' where the next one was coming from.' One must feel sorry, I think, for anyone who is powerless to help either himself or others ; and, while the merchantman is worse off, as he is bound to be the first target, my immediate thoughts could only be for our lads.

" Our R.A.F. crew, needless to say, are splendid. With all the excitement last night when I went aft, I hardly expected to find anyone at the winch. But there he was—our man who shall be nameless.

" **1155 hours.** This looks bad. About 30 Junker 87s with an escort of Messerschmitt 109s arrived over the convoy. The procedure is simple. The fighters try to put the balloons down in flames, and, like one platoon following another on the parade-ground, the dive-bombers follow. Whether they saw something we didn't, I don't know, but the bombers suddenly veered away and that was that. But not before our fighters had got a couple of Junkers and possibly a third.''

" **1845 hours.** Alongside quay. Tied up.''

The dive-bombers don't like them

One of the Convoy Balloon Officers also describes this most exciting aspect of balloon work.

" Now, as you know, the Navy are past-masters at escorting convoys ; they know every trick of the trade, and should Jerry's fertile imagination create some new situation which had not previously arisen, they would soon adapt themselves to deal with the novelty. One new situation that he has created, however, is that of the dive-bomber ; and whereas this method of attack is in no way confined to this stretch of water, it is certainly much more likely to be met with than in most other parts. Now a ship at sea, when all is said and done, is really a very small target, providing the attacking 'planes are not allowed to dive too low, and it is here that we of the Balloon Barrage do our bit.

" Each convoy is accompanied by vessels of the Royal Navy, carrying balloons : these are placed at vantage points amongst the convoy ; thus, in a sense, the escorted vessels are placed inside a box, with the Navy acting as the four walls of the box and the balloons acting as a lid. You may wonder how efficacious are these balloons in a dive-bombing attack. Actually I have never spoken to a German pilot so as to know what they think of them, but I have discussed the subject on many occasions with our own pilots and they have invariably told me that they hate them like hell, treat them with the greatest respect and avoid them like the plague. I must say, from my own personal experience, when Jerry has made an attack on us, he seems to concur with our own pilots' views, as invariably he sends Me.109s over first to attempt to shoot down the balloons, thereby making way for the dive-bombers following very close behind them.

" We have our own method of competing with those 109s, and it seems extremely effective ; on many occasions the bombers have arrived only to find all the balloons still flying, with the result that dive-bombing has to be turned into high-level bombing, which considerably reduces their accuracy. To give you some idea of what these trips are like, I want you to imagine that you are with us on one of the convoys. It is about tea-time and we are heading south towards the straits. The sun is setting over the English coast and we wallow along at a steady pre-arranged speed. The black and red colours of the merchant vessels are flanked by the sleek grey lines of the escort vessels. Overhead the silver of the balloons shines in the fading light. Every man is on the ' *qui vive*,' every gun is manned, and it would be idle to deny that we are all keyed up.

" Suddenly, out of the setting sun, three 'planes are spotted. Guns are trained on them, but our fire is held. Are they hostile or friendly ? In a matter of seconds there is a roar, and it is seen that each 'plane is diving at a different balloon. All our guns open fire and the dusk is lit up with hundreds of tracer bullets. By this time the 'planes are turning again from the east and preparing for a second attack ; once more they come, and once more hell is let loose from every ship. It is clear that the barrage from the escort vessels is too much for Jerry, and he makes off towards the French coast, having failed to destroy the balloons.

" Will you have your tea before the shelling ? "

" At this stage it is a safe bet that the dive-bombers are lurking not very far away ; and sure enough, in a very few minutes, there is a roar from a very great height as 8 or 16 or 24 planes swoop down on the convoy. But things have not gone according to their plans, for the balloons are still flying and the enemy cannot come low to drop their bombs. The German pilots must keep a weather eye on the balloons and the cables ; this upsets their accuracy, and their bombs fall harmlessly into the sea. Many of them fall extremely near to their objective, but direct hits have been turned into near misses and no damage is done. With a zoom the 'planes return to their bases—many of them, it is hoped, bearing scars to remind them of where they have been.

" For a moment the tension is relaxed. It is now nearly dark and we are approaching the straits. Not a light is to be seen, not a cigarette glows, as we creep on steadily, running according to schedule. At this stage we are more or less convinced that the big guns on the coast ought to have been informed of our approach. As the steward said to me on a recent trip, ' Will you have your tea served before the shelling or afterwards, sir ? ' The sun has completely gone, but the moon is throwing far too much light on the sea for our liking. The white cliffs of England can be clearly seen, and the searchlights light up the sky of the French coast.

" Suddenly large flashes are seen on the coast and streams of flaming onions rise out of the sky. More flashes follow, and we know that our Bomber Command are having their private party. Apparently no one is taking any notice of us : at least, we hope so. Then there is a loud crash, and a great column of water rises into the air some distance ahead on the port bow, and we know that the mine-sweepers are doing their work. By now we are in the narrowest part of the Straits. Flashes of bombs from the French coast, the stream of anti-aircraft tracers and the number of searchlights increase, while on the English coast searchlights leap into action as we hear 'planes pass overhead. Sometimes it seems that the search-lights from the two coasts almost meet above, while we, silent and unobserved, creep down the archway they form.

" Being optimists, we still believe nobody knows we are there : but this must be numbered among famous last hopes, for from the French coast four wicked yellow flashes light up the sky and we know that the guns on the French coast have started. The Commander on the bridge invariably turns round and says, ' Start counting, chaps ' ; and some 75 seconds later, four enormous crumps are heard and four great columns of water shoot up into the air. So it goes on, until the whole convoy has steamed out of range of the guns and we wait for any other surprises Jerry may have for us. I can tell you that it is a grand feeling when it is all over and one has the privilege of seeing the merchantmen, laden to their eyebrows, safely home, and knowing that Mr. Winston Churchill is right and that it *is* our Channel.''

*   *   *   *   *   *   *

There is little doubt that the ever-present barrage of balloons in the sky has been a great comfort to the population during aerial combat and bombardment. It has seemed, sometimes, particularly in fine weather, that the work of balloon operators was easy compared with that of other branches of the Royal Air Force. It is hoped that this short account has shown how the maintenance of an efficient balloon barrage, on such a vast scale as that which has been daily flown in the British Isles, demands high mental and physical alertness. Under fire, it is one of the most dangerous jobs ; in winter it is one of the coldest. At all times it is exacting.

Balloons in this war are not only scarecrows ; they have been scientifically distributed and devised as part of the defensive roof over the country. While they fly the enemy is not only denied the possibility of accurate bombing, but is also placed in a position of the greatest vulnerability to attack by anti-aircraft and fighter defences.

Postscript

THIS BOOK started with a story of inaction, and while it was being written there was another long, trying lull. After the last great attack on London in May 1941, nothing substantial happened for nearly a year. There were great scientific advances, but precious little chance to use them until the Baedeker raids. Though locally unpleasant, these raids were carried out by small bodies of about 50 bombers, and did not pretend to be anything except a peculiarly barbarous form of reprisal. The main reason why our smaller Cathedral cities were attacked seems to have been because, in the nature of things, they were likely to be the least well-equipped with

A.A. defences. In the military sense, these raids cannot be said to have interrupted the lull. They showed most satisfactorily, however, that the gunners had not wasted the respite.

On March 10th, 1941, south-coast gunners set up a record by shooting down four raiders in one night. A year later, when the raids came again, they shot down four in one hour. Two of these were brought down simultaneously. They were flying close together at a great height. At the first salvo they dived steeply, to be met by a second salvo. Then came a third. One raider blew up in mid-air and the other crashed into the sea in flames.

Another site of the same battery was awarded a share in the kill on each of the other two raiders brought down. The guns kept up a constant rate of fire of four shells per minute for over an hour. Working with the light A.A. unit, they engaged a low-flying raider, which blew up in mid-air. One bomb explosion blew two light A.A. gun-layers from their seats on the gun. They picked themselves up and jumped back. Six minutes later another enemy 'plane had been destroyed. This was also engaged by two other heavy gun sites and was shuttlecocked backwards and forwards, hit the sea twice, each time emitting flashes of flame, and then disappeared beneath the water. Good shooting!

There has, then, been no lull in the effort devoted to the improvement of our defences. If the *Luftwaffe*, baffled in the East, turns again to the West, it will find the opposition even stronger than that which baffled it here before. Meanwhile every part of the Air Defence of Great Britain can fairly claim its share in what history will undoubtedly pronounce to have been a victory. They baulked the German attempt to clear the way for invasion in the autumn of 1940. They frustrated the German attempt to break civilian morale through the long winter and spring of 1940–41. In this battle, Victory could not appear suddenly and dramatically. She edged her way almost imperceptibly on to the stage ; but she was there when the curtain fell. If and when it rises for a second act, she will be back in the wings and will have to be cajoled into appearing again.

There are many gaps in the story of this first Act. No actor must feel slighted that he is not mentioned by name. Those selected for mention among an immense cast were neither more gallant nor more successful than many of their colleagues. In a review of the play, such as this, all of so many similar parts could not be described, however much they all deserved description. It must be enough to record that the performance of all brought a worldwide audience to its feet.